The Thirty Yea

Volume 01

Friedrich Schiller

Alpha Editions

This edition published in 2023

ISBN : 9789357944380

Design and Setting By
Alpha Editions
www.alphaedis.com
Email - info@alphaedis.com

Contents

VOLUME 01

PREFACE TO THE SIXTH EDITION.

The present is the best collected edition of the important works of Schiller which is accessible to readers in the English language. Detached poems or dramas have been translated at various times since the first publication of the original works; and in several instances these versions have been incorporated into this collection. Schiller was not less efficiently qualified by nature for an historian than for a dramatist. He was formed to excel in all departments of literature, and the admirable lucidity of style and soundness and impartiality of judgment displayed in his historical writings will not easily be surpassed, and will always recommend them as popular expositions of the periods of which they treat.

Since the publication of the first English edition many corrections and improvements have been made, with a view to rendering it as acceptable as possible to English readers; and, notwithstanding the disadvantages of a translation, the publishers feel sure that Schiller will be heartily acceptable to English readers, and that the influence of his writings will continue to increase.

THE HISTORY OF THE REVOLT OF THE NETHERLANDS was translated by Lieut. E. B. Eastwick, and originally published abroad for students' use. But this translation was too strictly literal for general readers. It has been carefully revised, and some portions have been entirely rewritten by the Rev. A. J. W. Morrison, who also has so ably translated the HISTORY OF THE THIRTY YEARS WAR.

THE CAMP OF WALLENSTEIN was translated by Mr. James Churchill, and first appeared in "Frazer's Magazine." It is an exceedingly happy version of what has always been deemed the most untranslatable of Schiller's works.

THE PICCOLOMINI and DEATH OF WALLENSTEIN are the admirable version of S. T. Coleridge, completed by the addition of all those passages which he has omitted, and by a restoration of Schiller's own arrangement of the acts and scenes. It is said, in defence of the variations which exist between the German original and the version given by Coleridge, that he translated from a prompter's copy in manuscript, before the drama had been printed, and that Schiller himself subsequently altered it, by omitting some passages, adding others, and even engrafting several of Coleridge's adaptations.

WILHELM TELL is translated by Theodore Martin, Esq., whose well-known position as a writer, and whose special acquaintance with German literature make any recommendation superfluous.

DON CARLOS is translated by R. D. Boylan, Esq., and, in the opinion of competent judges, the version is eminently successful. Mr. Theodore Martin kindly gave some assistance, and, it is but justice to state, has enhanced the value of the work by his judicious suggestions.

The translation of MARY STUART is that by the late Joseph Mellish, who appears to have been on terms of intimate friendship with Schiller. His version was made from the prompter's copy, before the play was published, and, like Coleridge's Wallenstein, contains many passages not found in the printed edition. These are distinguished by brackets. On the other hand, Mr. Mellish omitted many passages which now form part of the printed drama, all of which are now added. The translation, as a whole, stands out from similar works of the time (1800) in almost as marked a degree as Coleridge's Wallenstein, and some passages exhibit powers of a high order; a few, however, especially in the earlier scenes, seemed capable of improvement, and these have been revised, but, in deference to the translator, with a sparing hand.

THE MAID OF ORLEANS is contributed by Miss Anna Swanwick, whose translation of Faust has since become well known. It has been. carefully revised, and is now, for the first time, published complete.

THE BRIDE OF MESSINA, which has been regarded as the poetical masterpiece of Schiller, and, perhaps of all his works, presents the greatest difficulties to the translator, is rendered by A. Lodge, Esq., M. A. This version, on its first publication in England, a few years ago, was received with deserved eulogy by distinguished critics. To the present edition has been prefixed Schiller's Essay on the Use of the Chorus in Tragedy, in which the author's favorite theory of the "Ideal of Art" is enforced with great ingenuity and eloquence.

BOOK I.

From the beginning of the religious wars in Germany, to the peace of Munster, scarcely any thing great or remarkable occurred in the political world of Europe in which the Reformation had not an important share. All the events of this period, if they did not originate in, soon became mixed up with, the question of religion, and no state was either too great or too little to feel directly or indirectly more or less of its influence.

Against the reformed doctrine and its adherents, the House of Austria directed, almost exclusively, the whole of its immense political power. In France, the Reformation had enkindled a civil war which, under four stormy reigns, shook the kingdom to its foundations, brought foreign armies into the heart of the country, and for half a century rendered it the scene of the most mournful disorders. It was the Reformation, too, that rendered the Spanish yoke intolerable to the Flemings, and awakened in them both the desire and the courage to throw off its fetters, while it also principally furnished them with the means of their emancipation. And as to England, all the evils with which Philip the Second threatened Elizabeth, were mainly intended in revenge for her having taken his Protestant subjects under her protection, and placing herself at the head of a religious party which it was his aim and endeavour to extirpate. In Germany, the schisms in the church produced also a lasting political schism, which made that country for more than a century the theatre of confusion, but at the same time threw up a firm barrier against political oppression. It was, too, the Reformation principally that first drew the northern powers, Denmark and Sweden, into the political system of Europe; and while on the one hand the Protestant League was strengthened by their adhesion, it on the other was indispensable to their interests. States which hitherto scarcely concerned themselves with one another's existence, acquired through the Reformation an attractive centre of interest, and began to be united by new political sympathies. And as through its influence new relations sprang up between citizen and citizen, and between rulers and subjects, so also entire states were forced by it into new relative positions. Thus, by a strange course of events, religious disputes were the means of cementing a closer union among the nations of Europe.

Fearful indeed, and destructive, was the first movement in which this general political sympathy announced itself; a desolating war of thirty years, which, from the interior of Bohemia to the mouth of the Scheldt, and from the banks of the Po to the coasts of the Baltic, devastated whole countries, destroyed harvests, and reduced towns and villages to ashes; which opened a grave for many thousand combatants, and for half a century smothered the glimmering sparks of civilization in Germany, and threw back the improving manners of the country into their pristine barbarity and wildness. Yet out of this fearful war Europe came forth free and independent. In it she first learned to recognize herself as a community of nations; and this intercommunion of states, which originated in the thirty years' war, may alone be sufficient to reconcile the philosopher to its horrors. The hand of industry has slowly but gradually effaced the traces of its ravages, while its beneficent influence still survives; and this general sympathy among the states of Europe, which grew out of the troubles in Bohemia, is our guarantee for the continuance of that peace which was the result of the war. As the sparks of destruction found their way from the interior of Bohemia, Moravia, and Austria, to kindle Germany, France, and the half of Europe, so also will the torch of civilization make a path for itself from the latter to enlighten the former countries.

All this was effected by religion. Religion alone could have rendered possible all that was accomplished, but it was far from being the SOLE motive of the war. Had not private advantages and state interests been closely connected with it, vain and powerless would have been the arguments of theologians; and the cry of the people would never have met with princes so willing to espouse their cause, nor the new doctrines have found such numerous, brave, and persevering champions. The Reformation is undoubtedly owing in a great measure to the invincible power of truth, or of opinions which were held as such. The abuses in the old church, the absurdity of many of its dogmas, the extravagance of its requisitions, necessarily revolted the tempers of men, already half-won with the promise of a better light, and favourably disposed them towards the new doctrines. The charm of independence, the rich plunder of monastic institutions, made the Reformation attractive in the eyes of princes, and tended not a little to strengthen their inward convictions. Nothing, however, but political considerations could have driven them to espouse it. Had not Charles the Fifth, in the intoxication of success, made an attempt on the independence of the German States, a Protestant league would scarcely have rushed to arms in defence of freedom of belief; but for the ambition of the Guises, the Calvinists in France would never have beheld a Conde or a Coligny at their head. Without the exaction of the tenth and the twentieth penny, the See of Rome had never lost the United Netherlands. Princes fought in self-defence or for aggrandizement, while religious enthusiasm recruited their armies, and opened to them the treasures of their subjects. Of the multitude who flocked to their standards, such as were not lured by the hope of plunder imagined they were fighting for the truth, while in fact they were shedding their blood for the personal objects of their princes.

And well was it for the people that, on this occasion, their interests coincided with those of their princes. To this coincidence alone were they indebted for their deliverance from popery. Well was it also for the rulers, that the subject contended too for his own cause, while he was fighting their battles. Fortunately at this date no European sovereign was so absolute as to be able, in the pursuit of his political designs, to dispense with the goodwill of his subjects. Yet how difficult was it to gain and to set to work this goodwill! The most impressive arguments drawn from reasons of state fall powerless on the ear of the subject, who seldom understands, and still more rarely is interested in them. In such circumstances, the only course open to a prudent prince is to connect the interests of the cabinet with some one that sits nearer to the people's heart, if such exists, or if not, to create it.

In such a position stood the greater part of those princes who embraced the cause of the Reformation. By a strange concatenation of events, the divisions of the Church were associated with two circumstances, without which, in all probability, they would have had a very different conclusion. These were, the increasing power of the House of Austria, which threatened the liberties of Europe, and its active zeal for the old religion. The first aroused the princes, while the second armed the people.

The abolition of a foreign jurisdiction within their own territories, the supremacy in ecclesiastical matters, the stopping of the treasure which had so long flowed to Rome, the rich plunder of religious foundations, were tempting advantages to every sovereign. Why, then, it may be asked, did they not operate with equal force upon the princes of the House of Austria? What prevented this house, particularly in its German branch, from yielding to the pressing demands of so many of its subjects, and, after the example of other princes, enriching itself at the expense of a defenceless clergy? It is difficult to credit that a belief in the infallibility of the Romish Church had any greater influence on the pious adherence of this house, than the opposite conviction had on the revolt of the Protestant princes. In fact, several circumstances combined to make the Austrian princes zealous supporters of popery. Spain and Italy, from which Austria derived its principal strength, were still devoted to the See of Rome with that blind obedience which, ever since the days of the Gothic dynasty, had been the peculiar characteristic of the Spaniard. The slightest approximation, in a Spanish prince, to the obnoxious tenets of Luther and Calvin, would have alienated for ever the affections of his subjects, and a defection from the Pope would have cost him the kingdom. A Spanish prince had no alternative but orthodoxy or abdication. The same restraint was imposed upon Austria by her Italian dominions, which she was obliged to treat, if possible, with even greater indulgence; impatient as they naturally were of a foreign yoke, and possessing also ready means of shaking it off. In regard to the latter provinces, moreover, the rival pretensions of France, and the neighbourhood of the Pope, were motives sufficient to prevent the Emperor from declaring in favour of a party which strove to annihilate the papal see, and also to induce him to show the most active zeal in behalf of the old religion. These general considerations, which must have been equally weighty with every Spanish monarch, were, in the particular case of Charles V., still further enforced by peculiar and personal motives. In Italy this monarch had a formidable rival in the King of France, under whose protection that country might throw itself the instant that Charles should incur the slightest suspicion of heresy. Distrust on the part of the Roman Catholics, and a rupture with the church, would have been fatal also to many of his most cherished designs. Moreover, when Charles was first called upon to make his election between the two parties, the new doctrine had not yet attained to a full and commanding influence, and there still subsisted a prospect of its reconciliation with the old. In his son and successor, Philip the Second, a monastic education combined with a gloomy and despotic disposition to generate an unmitigated hostility to all innovations in religion; a feeling which the thought that his most formidable political opponents were also the enemies of his faith was not calculated to weaken. As his European possessions, scattered as they were over so many countries, were on all sides exposed to the seductions of foreign opinions, the progress of the Reformation in other quarters could not well be a matter of indifference to him. His immediate interests, therefore, urged him to attach himself devotedly to the old church, in order to close up the sources of the heretical contagion. Thus, circumstances naturally placed this prince at the head of the league which the Roman Catholics formed against the Reformers. The principles which had actuated the long and active reigns of Charles V. and Philip the Second, remained a law for their successors; and the more the breach in the church widened, the firmer became the attachment of the Spaniards to Roman Catholicism.

The German line of the House of Austria was apparently more unfettered; but, in reality, though free from many of these restraints, it was yet confined by others. The possession of the imperial throne—a dignity it was impossible for a Protestant to hold, (for with what consistency could an apostate from the Romish Church wear the crown of a Roman emperor?) bound the successors of Ferdinand I. to the See of Rome. Ferdinand himself was, from conscientious motives, heartily attached to it. Besides, the German princes of the House of Austria were not powerful enough to dispense with the support of Spain, which, however, they would have forfeited by the least show of leaning towards the new doctrines. The imperial dignity, also, required them to preserve the existing political system of Germany, with which the maintenance of their own authority was closely bound up, but which it was the aim of the Protestant League to destroy. If to these grounds we add the indifference of the Protestants to the Emperor's necessities and to the common dangers of the empire, their encroachments on the temporalities of the church, and their aggressive violence when they became conscious of their own power, we can easily conceive how so many concurring motives must have determined the emperors to the side of popery, and how their own interests came to be intimately interwoven with those of the Roman Church. As its fate seemed to depend altogether on the part taken by Austria, the princes of this house came to be regarded by all Europe as the pillars of popery. The hatred, therefore, which the Protestants bore against the latter, was turned exclusively upon Austria; and the cause became gradually confounded with its protector.

But this irreconcileable enemy of the Reformation—the House of Austria —by its ambitious projects and the overwhelming force which it could bring to their support, endangered, in no small degree, the freedom of Europe, and more especially of the German States. This circumstance could not fail to rouse the latter from their security, and to render them vigilant in self-defence. Their ordinary resources were quite insufficient to resist so formidable a power. Extraordinary exertions were required from their subjects; and when even these proved far from adequate, they had recourse to foreign assistance; and, by means of a common league, they endeavoured to oppose a power which, singly, they were unable to withstand.

But the strong political inducements which the German princes had to resist the pretensions of the House of Austria, naturally did not extend to their subjects. It is only immediate advantages or immediate evils that set the people in action, and for these a sound policy cannot wait. Ill then would it have fared with these princes, if by good fortune another effectual motive had not offered itself, which roused the passions of the people, and kindled in them an enthusiasm which might be directed against the political danger, as having with it a common cause of alarm.

This motive was their avowed hatred of the religion which Austria protected, and their enthusiastic attachment to a doctrine which that House was endeavouring to extirpate by fire and sword. Their attachment was ardent, their hatred invincible. Religious fanaticism anticipates even the remotest dangers. Enthusiasm never calculates its sacrifices. What the most pressing danger of the state could not gain from the citizens, was effected by religious zeal. For the state, or for the prince, few would have drawn the sword; but for religion, the merchant, the artist, the peasant, all cheerfully flew to arms. For the state, or for the prince, even the smallest additional impost would have been avoided; but for religion the people readily staked at once life, fortune, and all earthly hopes. It trebled the contributions which flowed into the exchequer of the princes, and the armies which marched to the field; and, in the ardent excitement produced in all minds by the peril to which their faith was exposed, the subject felt not the pressure of those burdens and privations under which, in cooler moments, he would have sunk exhausted. The terrors of the Spanish Inquisition, and the massacre of St. Bartholomew's, procured for the Prince of Orange, the Admiral Coligny, the

British Queen Elizabeth, and the Protestant princes of Germany, supplies of men and money from their subjects, to a degree which at present is inconceivable.

But, with all their exertions, they would have effected little against a power which was an overmatch for any single adversary, however powerful. At this period of imperfect policy, accidental circumstances alone could determine distant states to afford one another a mutual support. The differences of government, of laws, of language, of manners, and of character, which hitherto had kept whole nations and countries as it were insulated, and raised a lasting barrier between them, rendered one state insensible to the distresses of another, save where national jealousy could indulge a malicious joy at the reverses of a rival. This barrier the Reformation destroyed. An interest more intense and more immediate than national aggrandizement or patriotism, and entirely independent of private utility, began to animate whole states and individual citizens; an interest capable of uniting numerous and distant nations, even while it frequently lost its force among the subjects of the same government. With the inhabitants of Geneva, for instance, of England, of Germany, or of Holland, the French Calvinist possessed a common point of union which he had not with his own countrymen. Thus, in one important particular, he ceased to be the citizen of a single state, and to confine his views and sympathies to his own country alone. The sphere of his views became enlarged. He began to calculate his own fate from that of other nations of the same religious profession, and to make their cause his own. Now for the first time did princes venture to bring the affairs of other countries before their own councils; for the first time could they hope for a willing ear to their own necessities, and prompt assistance from others. Foreign affairs had now become a matter of domestic policy, and that aid was readily granted to the religious confederate which would have been denied to the mere neighbour, and still more to the distant stranger. The inhabitant of the Palatinate leaves his native fields to fight side by side with his religious associate of France, against the common enemy of their faith. The Huguenot draws his sword against the country which persecutes him, and sheds his blood in defence of the liberties of Holland. Swiss is arrayed against Swiss; German against German, to determine, on the banks of the Loire and the Seine, the succession of the French crown. The Dane crosses the Eider, and the Swede the Baltic, to break the chains which are forged for Germany.

It is difficult to say what would have been the fate of the Reformation, and the liberties of the Empire, had not the formidable power of Austria declared against them. This, however, appears certain, that nothing so completely damped the Austrian hopes of universal monarchy, as the obstinate war which they had to wage against the new religious opinions. Under no other circumstances could the weaker princes have roused their subjects to such extraordinary exertions against the ambition of Austria, or the States themselves have united so closely against the common enemy.

The power of Austria never stood higher than after the victory which Charles V. gained over the Germans at Muehlberg. With the treaty of Smalcalde the freedom of Germany lay, as it seemed, prostrate for ever; but it revived under Maurice of Saxony, once its most formidable enemy. All the fruits of the victory of Muehlberg were lost again in the congress of Passau, and the diet of Augsburg; and every scheme for civil and religious oppression terminated in the concessions of an equitable peace.

The diet of Augsburg divided Germany into two religious and two political parties, by recognizing the independent rights and existence of both. Hitherto the Protestants had been looked on as rebels; they were henceforth to be regarded as brethren—not indeed through affection, but necessity. By the Interim, the Confession of Augsburg was allowed temporarily to take a sisterly place alongside of the olden religion, though only as a tolerated neighbour.

[A system of Theology so called, prepared by order of the Emperor Charles V. for the use of Germany, to reconcile the differences between the Roman Catholics and the Lutherans, which, however, was rejected by both parties—Ed.]

To every secular state was conceded the right of establishing the religion it acknowledged as supreme and exclusive within its own territories, and of forbidding the open profession of its rival. Subjects were to be free to quit a country where their own religion was not tolerated. The doctrines of Luther for the first time received a positive sanction; and if they were trampled under foot in Bavaria and Austria, they predominated in Saxony and Thuringia. But the sovereigns alone were to determine what form of religion should prevail within their territories; the feelings of subjects who had no representatives in the diet were little attended to in the pacification. In the ecclesiastical territories, indeed, where the unreformed religion enjoyed an undisputed supremacy, the free exercise of their religion was obtained for all who had previously embraced the Protestant doctrines; but this indulgence rested only on the personal guarantee of Ferdinand, King of the Romans, by whose endeavours chiefly this peace was effected; a guarantee, which, being rejected by the Roman Catholic members of the Diet, and only inserted in the treaty under their protest, could not of course have the force of law.

If it had been opinions only that thus divided the minds of men, with what indifference would all have regarded the division! But on these opinions depended riches, dignities, and rights; and it was this which so deeply aggravated the evils of division. Of two brothers, as it were, who had hitherto enjoyed a paternal inheritance in common, one now remained, while the other was compelled to leave his father's house, and hence arose the necessity of dividing the patrimony. For this separation, which he could not have foreseen, the father had made no provision. By the beneficent donations of pious ancestors the riches of the church had been accumulating through a thousand years, and these benefactors were as much the progenitors of the departing brother as of him who remained. Was the right of inheritance then to be limited to the paternal house, or to be extended to blood? The gifts had been made to the church in communion with Rome, because at that time no other existed,—to the first-born, as it were, because he was as yet the only son. Was then a right of primogeniture to be admitted in the church, as in noble families? Were the pretensions of one party to be favoured by a prescription from times when the claims of the other could not have come into existence? Could the Lutherans be justly excluded from these possessions, to which the benevolence of their forefathers had contributed, merely on the ground that, at the date of their foundation, the differences between Lutheranism and Romanism were unknown? Both parties have disputed, and still dispute, with equal plausibility, on these points. Both alike have found it difficult to prove their right. Law can be applied only to conceivable cases, and perhaps spiritual foundations are not among the number of these, and still less where the conditions of the founders generally extended to a system of doctrines; for how is it conceivable that a permanent endowment should be made of opinions left open to change?

What law cannot decide, is usually determined by might, and such was the case here. The one party held firmly all that could no longer be wrested from it—the other defended what it still possessed. All the bishoprics and abbeys which had been secularized BEFORE the peace, remained with the Protestants; but, by an express clause, the unreformed Catholics provided that none should thereafter be secularized. Every impropriator of an ecclesiastical foundation, who held immediately of the Empire, whether elector, bishop, or abbot, forfeited his benefice and dignity the moment he embraced the Protestant belief; he was obliged in that event instantly to resign its emoluments, and the chapter was to proceed to a new election, exactly as if his place had been vacated by death. By this sacred anchor of the Ecclesiastical Reservation, (`Reservatum Ecclesiasticum',) which makes the temporal existence of a spiritual prince entirely dependent on his fidelity to the olden religion, the Roman Catholic Church in Germany is still held fast; and precarious, indeed, would be its situation were this anchor to give way. The principle of the Ecclesiastical Reservation was strongly opposed by the Protestants; and though it was at last adopted into the treaty of peace, its insertion was qualified with the declaration, that parties had come to no final determination on the point. Could it then be more binding on the Protestants than Ferdinand's guarantee in favour of Protestant subjects of ecclesiastical states was upon the Roman Catholics? Thus were two important subjects of dispute left unsettled in the treaty of peace, and by them the war was rekindled.

Such was the position of things with regard to religious toleration and ecclesiastical property: it was the same with regard to rights and dignities. The existing German system provided only for one church, because one only was in existence when that system was framed. The church had now divided; the Diet had broken into two religious parties; was the whole system of the Empire still exclusively to follow the one? The emperors had hitherto been members of the Romish Church, because till now that religion had no rival. But was it his connexion with Rome which constituted a German emperor, or was it not rather Germany which was to be represented in its head? The Protestants were now spread over the whole Empire, and how could they justly still be represented by an unbroken line of Roman Catholic emperors? In the Imperial Chamber the German States judge themselves, for they elect the judges; it was the very end of its institution that they should do so, in order that equal justice should be dispensed to all; but would this be still possible, if the representatives of both professions were not equally admissible to a seat in the Chamber? That one religion only existed in Germany at the time of its establishment, was accidental; that no one estate should have the means of legally oppressing another, was the essential purpose of the institution. Now this object would be entirely frustrated if one religious party were to have the exclusive power of deciding for the other. Must, then, the design be sacrificed, because that which was merely accidental had changed? With great difficulty the Protestants, at last, obtained for the representatives of their religion a place in the Supreme Council, but still there was far from being a perfect equality of voices. To this day no Protestant prince has been raised to the imperial throne.

Whatever may be said of the equality which the peace of Augsburg was to have established between the two German churches, the Roman Catholic had unquestionably still the advantage. All that the Lutheran Church gained by it was toleration; all that the Romish Church conceded, was a sacrifice to necessity, not an offering to justice. Very far was it from being a peace between two equal powers, but a truce between a sovereign and unconquered rebels. From this principle all the proceedings of the Roman Catholics against the Protestants seemed to flow, and still continue to do so. To join the reformed faith was still a crime, since it was to be visited with so severe a penalty as that which the Ecclesiastical Reservation held suspended over the apostacy of the spiritual princes. Even to the last, the Romish Church preferred to risk to loss of every thing by force, than voluntarily to yield the smallest matter to justice. The loss was accidental and might be repaired; but the abandonment of its pretensions, the concession of a single point to the

Protestants, would shake the foundations of the church itself. Even in the treaty of peace this principle was not lost sight of. Whatever in this peace was yielded to the Protestants was always under condition. It was expressly declared, that affairs were to remain on the stipulated footing only till the next general council, which was to be called with the view of effecting an union between the two confessions. Then only, when this last attempt should have failed, was the religious treaty to become valid and conclusive. However little hope there might be of such a reconciliation, however little perhaps the Romanists themselves were in earnest with it, still it was something to have clogged the peace with these stipulations.

Thus this religious treaty, which was to extinguish for ever the flames of civil war, was, in fact, but a temporary truce, extorted by force and necessity; not dictated by justice, nor emanating from just notions either of religion or toleration. A religious treaty of this kind the Roman Catholics were as incapable of granting, to be candid, as in truth the Lutherans were unqualified to receive. Far from evincing a tolerant spirit towards the Roman Catholics, when it was in their power, they even oppressed the Calvinists; who indeed just as little deserved toleration, since they were unwilling to practise it. For such a peace the times were not yet ripe—the minds of men not yet sufficiently enlightened. How could one party expect from another what itself was incapable of performing? What each side saved or gained by the treaty of Augsburg, it owed to the imposing attitude of strength which it maintained at the time of its negociation. What was won by force was to be maintained also by force; if the peace was to be permanent, the two parties to it must preserve the same relative positions. The boundaries of the two churches had been marked out with the sword; with the sword they must be preserved, or woe to that party which should be first disarmed! A sad and fearful prospect for the tranquillity of Germany, when peace itself bore so threatening an aspect.

A momentary lull now pervaded the empire; a transitory bond of concord appeared to unite its scattered limbs into one body, so that for a time a feeling also for the common weal returned. But the division had penetrated its inmost being, and to restore its original harmony was impossible. Carefully as the treaty of peace appeared to have defined the rights of both parties, its interpretation was nevertheless the subject of many disputes. In the heat of conflict it had produced a cessation of hostilities; it covered, not extinguished, the fire, and unsatisfied claims remained on either side. The Romanists imagined they had lost too much, the Protestants that they had gained too little; and the treaty which neither party could venture to violate, was interpreted by each in its own favour.

The seizure of the ecclesiastical benefices, the motive which had so strongly tempted the majority of the Protestant princes to embrace the doctrines of

Luther, was not less powerful after than before the peace; of those whose founders had not held their fiefs immediately of the empire, such as were not already in their possession would it was evident soon be so. The whole of Lower Germany was already secularized; and if it were otherwise in Upper Germany, it was owing to the vehement resistance of the Catholics, who had there the preponderance. Each party, where it was the most powerful, oppressed the adherents of the other; the ecclesiastical princes in particular, as the most defenceless members of the empire, were incessantly tormented by the ambition of their Protestant neighbours. Those who were too weak to repel force by force, took refuge under the wings of justice; and the complaints of spoliation were heaped up against the Protestants in the Imperial Chamber, which was ready enough to pursue the accused with judgments, but found too little support to carry them into effect. The peace which stipulated for complete religious toleration for the dignitaries of the Empire, had provided also for the subject, by enabling him, without interruption, to leave the country in which the exercise of his religion was prohibited. But from the wrongs which the violence of a sovereign might inflict on an obnoxious subject; from the nameless oppressions by which he might harass and annoy the emigrant; from the artful snares in which subtilty combined with power might enmesh him—from these, the dead letter of the treaty could afford him no protection. The Catholic subject of Protestant princes complained loudly of violations of the religious peace—the Lutherans still more loudly of the oppression they experienced under their Romanist suzerains. The rancour and animosities of theologians infused a poison into every occurrence, however inconsiderable, and inflamed the minds of the people. Happy would it have been had this theological hatred exhausted its zeal upon the common enemy, instead of venting its virus on the adherents of a kindred faith!

Unanimity amongst the Protestants might, by preserving the balance between the contending parties, have prolonged the peace; but as if to complete the confusion, all concord was quickly broken. The doctrines which had been propagated by Zuingli in Zurich, and by Calvin in Geneva, soon spread to Germany, and divided the Protestants among themselves, with little in unison save their common hatred to popery. The Protestants of this date bore but slight resemblance to those who, fifty years before, drew up the Confession of Augsburg; and the cause of the change is to be sought in that Confession itself. It had prescribed a positive boundary to the Protestant faith, before the newly awakened spirit of inquiry had satisfied itself as to the limits it ought to set; and the Protestants seemed unwittingly to have thrown away much of the advantage acquired by their rejection of popery. Common complaints of the Romish hierarchy, and of ecclesiastical abuses, and a common disapprobation of its dogmas, formed a sufficient centre of union for the Protestants; but not content with this, they sought a rallying point in the promulgation of a new and positive creed, in which they sought to embody the distinctions, the privileges, and the essence of the church, and to this they referred the convention entered into with their opponents. It was as professors of this creed that they had acceded to the treaty; and in the benefits of this peace the advocates of the confession were alone entitled to participate. In any case, therefore, the situation of its adherents was embarrassing. If a blind obedience were yielded to the dicta of the Confession, a lasting bound would be set to the spirit of inquiry; if, on the other hand, they dissented from the formulae agreed upon, the point of union would be lost. Unfortunately both incidents occurred, and the evil results of both were quickly felt. One party rigorously adhered to the original symbol of faith, and the other abandoned it, only to adopt another with equal exclusiveness.

Nothing could have furnished the common enemy a more plausible defence of his cause than this dissension; no spectacle could have been more gratifying to him than the rancour with which the Protestants alternately persecuted each other. Who could condemn the Roman Catholics, if they laughed at the audacity with which the Reformers had presumed to announce the only true belief?—if from Protestants they borrowed the weapons against Protestants?—if, in the midst of this clashing of opinions, they held fast to the authority of their own church, for which, in part, there spoke an honourable antiquity, and a yet more honourable plurality of voices. But this division placed the Protestants in still more serious embarrassments. As the covenants of the treaty applied only to the partisans of the Confession, their opponents, with some reason, called upon them to explain who were to be recognized as the adherents of that creed. The Lutherans could not, without offending conscience, include the Calvinists in their communion, except at the risk of converting a useful friend into a dangerous enemy, could they exclude them. This unfortunate difference opened a way for the machinations of the Jesuits to sow distrust between both parties, and to destroy the unity of their measures. Fettered by the double fear of their direct adversaries, and of their opponents among themselves, the Protestants lost for ever the opportunity of placing their church on a perfect equality with the Catholic. All these difficulties would have been avoided, and the defection of the Calvinists would not have prejudiced the common cause, if the point of union had been placed simply in the abandonment of Romanism, instead of in the Confession of Augsburg.

But however divided on other points, they concurred in this—that the security which had resulted from equality of power could only be maintained by the preservation of that balance. In the meanwhile, the continual reforms of one party, and the opposing measures of the other, kept both upon the watch, while the interpretation of the religious treaty was a never-ending subject of dispute. Each party maintained that every step taken by its opponent was an infraction of the peace, while of every movement of its own it was asserted that it was essential to its maintenance. Yet all the measures of the Catholics did not, as their opponents alleged, proceed from a spirit of encroachment—many of them were the necessary precautions of self-defence. The Protestants had shown unequivocally enough what the Romanists might expect if they were unfortunate enough to become the weaker party. The greediness of the former for the property of the church, gave no reason to expect indulgence;—their bitter hatred left no hope of magnanimity or forbearance.

But the Protestants, likewise, were excusable if they too placed little confidence in the sincerity of the Roman Catholics. By the treacherous and inhuman treatment which their brethren in Spain, France, and the Netherlands, had suffered; by the disgraceful subterfuge of the Romish princes, who held that the Pope had power to relieve them from the obligation of the most solemn oaths; and above all, by the detestable maxim, that faith was not to be kept with heretics, the Roman Church, in the eyes of all honest men, had lost its honour. No engagement, no oath, however sacred, from a Roman Catholic, could satisfy a Protestant. What security then could the religious peace afford, when, throughout Germany, the Jesuits represented it as a measure of mere temporary convenience, and in Rome itself it was solemnly repudiated.

The General Council, to which reference had been made in the treaty, had already been held in the city of Trent; but, as might have been foreseen, without accommodating the religious differences, or taking a single step to effect such accommodation, and even without being attended by the Protestants. The latter, indeed, were now solemnly excommunicated by it in the name of the church, whose representative the Council gave itself out to be. Could, then, a secular treaty, extorted moreover by force of arms, afford them adequate protection against the ban of the church; a treaty, too, based on a condition which the decision of the Council seemed entirely to abolish? There was then a show of right for violating the peace, if only the Romanists possessed the power; and henceforward the Protestants were protected by nothing but the respect for their formidable array.

Other circumstances combined to augment this distrust. Spain, on whose support the Romanists in Germany chiefly relied, was engaged in a bloody conflict with the Flemings. By it, the flower of the Spanish troops were drawn to the confines of Germany. With what ease might they be introduced within the empire, if a decisive stroke should render their presence necessary? Germany was at that time a magazine of war for nearly all the powers of Europe. The religious war had crowded it with soldiers, whom the peace left destitute; its many independent princes found it easy to assemble armies, and afterwards, for the sake of gain, or the interests of party, hire them out to other powers. With German troops, Philip the Second waged war against the Netherlands, and with German troops they defended themselves. Every such levy in Germany was a subject of alarm to the one party or the other, since it might be intended for their oppression. The arrival of an ambassador, an extraordinary legate of the Pope, a conference of princes, every unusual incident, must, it was thought, be pregnant with destruction to some party. Thus, for nearly half a century, stood Germany, her hand upon the sword; every rustle of a leaf alarmed her.

Ferdinand the First, King of Hungary, and his excellent son, Maximilian the Second, held at this memorable epoch the reins of government. With a heart full of sincerity, with a truly heroic patience, had Ferdinand brought about the religious peace of Augsburg, and afterwards, in the Council of Trent, laboured assiduously, though vainly, at the ungrateful task of reconciling the two religions. Abandoned by his nephew, Philip of Spain, and hard pressed both in Hungary and Transylvania by the victorious armies of the Turks, it was not likely that this emperor would entertain the idea of violating the religious peace, and thereby destroying his own painful work. The heavy expenses of the perpetually recurring war with Turkey could not be defrayed by the meagre contributions of his exhausted hereditary dominions. He stood, therefore, in need of the assistance of the whole empire; and the religious peace alone preserved in one body the otherwise divided empire. Financial necessities made the Protestant as needful to him as the Romanist, and imposed upon him the obligation of treating both parties with equal justice, which, amidst so many contradictory claims, was truly a colossal task. Very far, however, was the result from answering his expectations. His indulgence of the Protestants served only to bring upon his successors a war, which death saved himself the mortification of witnessing. Scarcely more fortunate was his son Maximilian, with whom perhaps the pressure of circumstances was the only obstacle, and a longer life perhaps the only want, to his establishing the new religion upon the imperial throne. Necessity had taught the father forbearance towards the Protestants—necessity and justice dictated the same course to the son. The grandson had reason to repent that he neither listened to justice, nor yielded to necessity.

Maximilian left six sons, of whom the eldest, the Archduke Rodolph, inherited his dominions, and ascended the imperial throne. The other brothers were put off with petty appanages. A few mesne fiefs were held by a collateral branch, which had their uncle, Charles of Styria, at its head; and even these were afterwards, under his son, Ferdinand the Second, incorporated with the rest of the family dominions. With this exception, the whole of the imposing power of Austria was now wielded by a single, but unfortunately weak hand.

Rodolph the Second was not devoid of those virtues which might have gained him the esteem of mankind, had the lot of a private station fallen to him. His character was mild, he loved peace and the sciences, particularly astronomy, natural history, chemistry, and the study of antiquities. To these he applied with a passionate zeal, which, at the very time when the critical posture of affairs demanded all his attention, and his exhausted finances the most rigid economy, diverted his attention from state affairs, and involved him in pernicious expenses. His taste for astronomy soon lost itself in those astrological reveries to which timid and melancholy temperaments like his are but too disposed. This, together with a youth passed in Spain, opened his ears to the evil counsels of the Jesuits, and the influence of the Spanish court, by which at last he was wholly governed. Ruled by tastes so little in accordance with the dignity of his station, and alarmed by ridiculous prophecies, he withdrew, after the Spanish custom, from the eyes of his subjects, to bury himself amidst his gems and antiques, or to make experiments in his laboratory, while the most fatal discords loosened all the bands of the empire, and the flames of rebellion began to burst out at the very footsteps of his throne. All access to his person was denied, the most urgent matters were neglected. The prospect of the rich inheritance of Spain was closed against him, while he was trying to make up his mind to offer his hand to the Infanta Isabella. A fearful anarchy threatened the Empire, for though without an heir of his own body, he could not be persuaded to allow the election of a King of the Romans. The Austrian States renounced their allegiance, Hungary and Transylvania threw off his supremacy, and Bohemia was not slow in following their example. The descendant of the once so formidable Charles the Fifth was in perpetual danger, either of losing one part of his possessions to the Turks, or another to the Protestants, and of sinking, beyond redemption, under the formidable coalition which a great monarch of Europe had formed against him. The events which now took place in the interior of Germany were such as usually happened when either the throne was without an emperor, or the Emperor without a sense of his imperial dignity. Outraged or abandoned by their head, the States of the Empire were left to help themselves; and alliances among themselves must supply the defective authority of the Emperor. Germany was divided into two leagues, which stood in arms arrayed against each other: between both, Rodolph, the despised opponent of the one, and the impotent protector of the other, remained irresolute and useless, equally unable to destroy the former or to command the latter. What had the Empire to look for from a prince incapable even of defending his hereditary dominions against its domestic enemies? To prevent the utter ruin of the House of Austria, his own family combined against him; and a powerful party threw itself into the arms of his brother. Driven from his hereditary dominions, nothing was now left him to lose but the imperial dignity; and he was only spared this last disgrace by a timely death.

At this critical moment, when only a supple policy, united with a vigorous arm, could have maintained the tranquillity of the Empire, its evil genius gave it a Rodolph for Emperor. At a more peaceful period the Germanic Union would have managed its own interests, and Rodolph, like so many others of his rank, might have hidden his deficiencies in a mysterious obscurity. But the urgent demand for the qualities in which he was most deficient revealed his incapacity. The position of Germany called for an emperor who, by his known energies, could give weight to his resolves; and the hereditary dominions of Rodolph, considerable as they were, were at present in a situation to occasion the greatest embarrassment to the governors.

The Austrian princes, it is true were Roman Catholics, and in addition to that, the supporters of Popery, but their countries were far from being so. The reformed opinions had penetrated even these, and favoured by Ferdinand's necessities and Maximilian's mildness, had met with a rapid success. The Austrian provinces exhibited in miniature what Germany did on a larger scale. The great nobles and the ritter class or knights were chiefly evangelical, and in the cities the Protestants had a decided preponderance. If they succeeded in bringing a few of their party into the country, they contrived imperceptibly to fill all places of trust and the magistracy with their own adherents, and to exclude the Catholics. Against the numerous order of the nobles and knights, and the deputies from the towns, the voice of a few prelates was powerless; and the unseemly ridicule and offensive contempt of the former soon drove them entirely from the provincial diets. Thus the whole of the Austrian Diet had imperceptibly become Protestant, and the Reformation was making rapid strides towards its public recognition. The prince was dependent on the Estates, who had it in their power to grant or refuse supplies. Accordingly, they availed themselves of the financial necessities of Ferdinand and his son to extort one religious concession after another. To the nobles and knights, Maximilian at last conceded the free exercise of their religion, but only within their own territories and castles. The intemperate enthusiasm of the Protestant preachers overstepped the boundaries which prudence had prescribed. In defiance of the express prohibition, several of them ventured to preach publicly, not only in the towns, but in Vienna itself, and the people flocked in crowds to this new doctrine, the best seasoning of which was personality and abuse. Thus continued food was supplied to fanaticism, and the hatred of two churches, that were such near neighbours, was farther envenomed by the sting of an impure zeal.

Among the hereditary dominions of the House of Austria, Hungary and Transylvania were the most unstable, and the most difficult to retain. The impossibility of holding these two countries against the neighbouring and overwhelming power of the Turks, had already driven Ferdinand to the inglorious expedient of recognizing, by an annual tribute, the Porte's supremacy over Transylvania; a shameful confession of weakness, and a still more dangerous temptation to the turbulent nobility, when they fancied they had any reason to complain of their master. Not without conditions had the Hungarians submitted to the House of Austria. They asserted the elective freedom of their crown, and boldly contended for all those prerogatives of their order which are inseparable from this freedom of election. The near neighbourhood of Turkey, the facility of changing masters with impunity, encouraged the magnates still more in their presumption; discontented with the Austrian government they threw themselves into the arms of the Turks; dissatisfied with these, they returned again to their German sovereigns. The frequency and rapidity of these transitions from one government to another, had communicated its influences also to their mode of thinking; and as their country wavered between the Turkish and Austrian rule, so their minds vacillated between revolt and submission. The more unfortunate each nation felt itself in being degraded into a province of a foreign kingdom, the stronger desire did they feel to obey a monarch chosen from amongst themselves, and thus it was always easy for an enterprising noble to obtain their support. The nearest Turkish pasha was always ready to bestow the Hungarian sceptre and crown on a rebel against Austria; just as ready was Austria to confirm to any adventurer the possession of provinces which he had wrested from the Porte, satisfied with preserving thereby the shadow of authority, and with erecting at the same time a barrier against the Turks. In this way several of these magnates, Batbori, Boschkai, Ragoczi, and Bethlen succeeded in establishing themselves, one after another, as tributary sovereigns in Transylvania and Hungary; and they maintained their ground by no deeper policy than that of occasionally joining the enemy, in order to render themselves more formidable to their own prince.

Ferdinand, Maximilian, and Rodolph, who were all sovereigns of Hungary and Transylvania, exhausted their other territories in endeavouring to defend these from the hostile inroads of the Turks, and to put down intestine rebellion. In this quarter destructive wars were succeeded but by brief truces, which were scarcely less hurtful: far and wide the land lay waste, while the injured serf had to complain equally of his enemy and his protector. Into these countries also the Reformation had penetrated; and protected by the freedom of the States, and under the cover of the internal disorders, had made a noticeable progress. Here too it was incautiously attacked, and party spirit thus became yet more dangerous from religious enthusiasm. Headed by a bold rebel, Boschkai, the nobles of Hungary and Transylvania raised the standard of rebellion. The Hungarian insurgents were upon the point of making common cause with the discontented Protestants in Austria,

Moravia, and Bohemia, and uniting all those countries in one fearful revolt. The downfall of popery in these lands would then have been inevitable.

Long had the Austrian archdukes, the brothers of the Emperor, beheld with silent indignation the impending ruin of their house; this last event hastened their decision. The Archduke Matthias, Maximilian's second son, Viceroy in Hungary, and Rodolph's presumptive heir, now came forward as the stay of the falling house of Hapsburg. In his youth, misled by a false ambition, this prince, disregarding the interests of his family, had listened to the overtures of the Flemish insurgents, who invited him into the Netherlands to conduct the defence of their liberties against the oppression of his own relative, Philip the Second. Mistaking the voice of an insulated faction for that of the entire nation, Matthias obeyed the call. But the event answered the expectations of the men of Brabant as little as his own, and from this imprudent enterprise he retired with little credit.

Far more honourable was his second appearance in the political world. Perceiving that his repeated remonstrances with the Emperor were unavailing, he assembled the archdukes, his brothers and cousins, at Presburg, and consulted with them on the growing perils of their house, when they unanimously assigned to him, as the oldest, the duty of defending that patrimony which a feeble brother was endangering. In his hands they placed all their powers and rights, and vested him with sovereign authority, to act at his discretion for the common good. Matthias immediately opened a communication with the Porte and the Hungarian rebels, and through his skilful management succeeded in saving, by a peace with the Turks, the remainder of Hungary, and by a treaty with the rebels, preserved the claims of Austria to the lost provinces. But Rodolph, as jealous as he had hitherto been careless of his sovereign authority, refused to ratify this treaty, which he regarded as a criminal encroachment on his sovereign rights. He accused the Archduke of keeping up a secret understanding with the enemy, and of cherishing treasonable designs on the crown of Hungary.

The activity of Matthias was, in truth, anything but disinterested; the conduct of the Emperor only accelerated the execution of his ambitious views. Secure, from motives of gratitude, of the devotion of the Hungarians, for whom he had so lately obtained the blessings of peace; assured by his agents of the favourable disposition of the nobles, and certain of the support of a large party, even in Austria, he now ventured to assume a bolder attitude, and, sword in hand, to discuss his grievances with the Emperor. The Protestants in Austria and Moravia, long ripe for revolt, and now won over to the Archduke by his promises of toleration, loudly and openly espoused his cause, and their long-menaced alliance with the Hungarian rebels was actually effected. Almost at once a formidable conspiracy was planned and matured against the Emperor. Too late did he resolve to amend his past errors; in vain did he attempt to break up this fatal alliance. Already the whole empire was in arms; Hungary, Austria, and Moravia had done homage to Matthias, who was already on his march to Bohemia to seize the Emperor in his palace, and to cut at once the sinews of his power.

Bohemia was not a more peaceable possession for Austria than Hungary; with this difference only, that, in the latter, political considerations, in the former, religious dissensions, fomented disorders. In Bohemia, a century before the days of Luther, the first spark of the religious war had been kindled; a century after Luther, the first flames of the thirty years' war burst out in Bohemia. The sect which owed its rise to John Huss, still existed in that country;—it agreed with the Romish Church in ceremonies and doctrines, with the single exception of the administration of the Communion, in which the Hussites communicated in both kinds. This privilege had been conceded to the followers of Huss by the Council of Basle, in an express treaty, (the Bohemian Compact); and though it was afterwards disavowed by the popes, they nevertheless continued to profit by it under the sanction of the government. As the use of the cup formed the only important distinction of their body, they were usually designated by the name of Utraquists; and they readily adopted an appellation which reminded them of their dearly valued privilege. But under this title lurked also the far stricter sects of the Bohemian and Moravian Brethren, who differed from the predominant church in more important particulars, and bore, in fact, a great resemblance to the German Protestants. Among them both, the German and Swiss opinions on religion made rapid progress; while the name of Utraquists, under which they managed to disguise the change of their principles, shielded them from persecution.

In truth, they had nothing in common with the Utraquists but the name; essentially, they were altogether Protestant. Confident in the strength of their party, and the Emperor's toleration under Maximilian, they had openly avowed their tenets. After the example of the Germans, they drew up a Confession of their own, in which Lutherans as well as Calvinists recognized their own doctrines, and they sought to transfer to the new Confession the privileges of the original Utraquists. In this they were opposed by their Roman Catholic countrymen, and forced to rest content with the Emperor's verbal assurance of protection.

As long as Maximilian lived, they enjoyed complete toleration, even under the new form they had taken. Under his successor the scene changed. An imperial edict appeared, which deprived the Bohemian Brethren of their religious freedom. Now these differed in nothing from the other Utraquists. The sentence, therefore, of their condemnation, obviously included all the partisans of the Bohemian Confession. Accordingly, they all combined to oppose the imperial mandate in the Diet, but without being able to procure its revocation. The Emperor and the Roman Catholic Estates took their ground on the Compact and the Bohemian Constitution; in which nothing appeared in favour of a religion which had not then obtained the voice of the country. Since that time, how completely had affairs changed! What then formed but an inconsiderable opinion, had now become the predominant religion of the country. And what was it then, but a subterfuge to limit a newly spreading religion by the terms of obsolete treaties? The Bohemian Protestants appealed to the verbal guarantee of Maximilian, and the religious freedom of the Germans, with whom they argued they ought to be on a footing of equality. It was in vain—their appeal was dismissed.

Such was the posture of affairs in Bohemia, when Matthias, already master of Hungary, Austria, and Moravia, appeared in Kolin, to raise the Bohemian Estates also against the Emperor. The embarrassment of the latter was now at its height. Abandoned by all his other subjects, he placed his last hopes on the Bohemians, who, it might be foreseen, would take advantage of his necessities to enforce their own demands. After an interval of many years, he once more appeared publicly in the Diet at Prague; and to convince the people that he was really still in existence, orders were given that all the windows should be opened in the streets through which he was to pass—proof enough how far things had gone with him. The event justified his fears. The Estates, conscious of their own power, refused to take a single step until their privileges were confirmed, and religious toleration fully assured to them. It was in vain to have recourse now to the old system of evasion. The Emperor's fate was in their hands, and he must yield to necessity. At present, however, he only granted their other demands—religious matters he reserved for consideration at the next Diet.

The Bohemians now took up arms in defence of the Emperor, and a bloody war between the two brothers was on the point of breaking out. But Rodolph, who feared nothing so much as remaining in this slavish dependence on the Estates, waited not for a warlike issue, but hastened to effect a reconciliation with his brother by more peaceable means. By a formal act of abdication he resigned to Matthias, what indeed he had no chance of wresting from him, Austria and the kingdom of Hungary, and acknowledged him as his successor to the crown of Bohemia.

Dearly enough had the Emperor extricated himself from one difficulty, only to get immediately involved in another. The settlement of the religious affairs of Bohemia had been referred to the next Diet, which was held in 1609. The reformed Bohemians demanded the free exercise of their faith, as under the former emperors; a Consistory of their own; the cession of the University of Prague; and the right of electing `Defenders', or `Protectors' of `Liberty', from their own body. The answer was the same as before; for the timid Emperor was now entirely fettered by the unreformed party. However often, and in however threatening language the Estates renewed their remonstrances, the Emperor persisted in his first declaration of granting nothing beyond the old compact. The Diet broke up without coming to a decision; and the Estates, exasperated against the Emperor, arranged a general meeting at Prague, upon their own authority, to right themselves.

They appeared at Prague in great force. In defiance of the imperial prohibition, they carried on their deliberations almost under the very eyes of the Emperor. The yielding compliance which he began to show, only proved how much they were feared, and increased their audacity. Yet on the main point he remained inflexible. They fulfilled their threats, and at last resolved to establish, by their own power, the free and universal exercise of their religion, and to abandon the Emperor to his necessities until he should confirm this resolution. They even went farther, and elected for themselves the DEFENDERS which the Emperor had refused them. Ten were nominated by each of the three Estates; they also determined to raise, as soon as possible, an armed force, at the head of which Count Thurn, the chief organizer of the revolt, should be placed as general defender of the liberties of Bohemia. Their determination brought the Emperor to submission, to which he was now counselled even by the Spaniards. Apprehensive lest the exasperated Estates should throw themselves into the arms of the King of Hungary, he signed the memorable Letter of Majesty for Bohemia, by which, under the successors of the Emperor, that people justified their rebellion.

The Bohemian Confession, which the States had laid before the Emperor Maximilian, was, by the Letter of Majesty, placed on a footing of equality with the olden profession. The Utraquists, for by this title the Bohemian Protestants continued to designate themselves, were put in possession of the University of Prague, and allowed a Consistory of their own, entirely independent of the archiepiscopal see of that city. All the churches in the cities, villages, and market towns, which they held at the date of the letter, were secured to them; and if in addition they wished to erect others, it was permitted to the nobles, and knights, and the free cities to do so. This last clause in the Letter of Majesty gave rise to the unfortunate disputes which subsequently rekindled the flames of war in Europe.

The Letter of Majesty erected the Protestant part of Bohemia into a kind of republic. The Estates had learned to feel the power which they gained by perseverance, unity, and harmony in their measures. The Emperor now retained little more than the shadow of his sovereign authority; while by the new dignity of the so-called defenders of liberty, a dangerous stimulus was given to the spirit of revolt. The example and success of Bohemia afforded a tempting seduction to the other hereditary dominions of Austria, and all attempted by similar means to extort similar privileges. The spirit of liberty spread from one province to another; and as it was chiefly the disunion among the Austrian princes that had enabled the Protestants so materially to improve their advantages, they now hastened to effect a reconciliation between the Emperor and the King of Hungary.

But the reconciliation could not be sincere. The wrong was too great to be forgiven, and Rodolph continued to nourish at heart an unextinguishable hatred of Matthias. With grief and indignation he brooded over the thought, that the Bohemian sceptre was finally to descend into the hands of his enemy; and the prospect was not more consoling, even if Matthias should die without issue. In that case, Ferdinand, Archduke of Graetz, whom he equally disliked, was the head of the family. To exclude the latter as well as Matthias from the succession to the throne of Bohemia, he fell upon the project of diverting that inheritance to Ferdinand's brother, the Archduke Leopold, Bishop of Passau, who among all his relatives had ever been the dearest and most deserving. The prejudices of the Bohemians in favour of the elective freedom of their crown, and their attachment to Leopold's person, seemed to favour this scheme, in which Rodolph consulted rather his own partiality and vindictiveness than the good of his house. But to carry out this project, a military force was requisite, and Rodolph actually assembled an army in the bishopric of Passau. The object of this force was hidden from all. An inroad, however, which, for want of pay it made suddenly and without the Emperor's knowledge into Bohemia, and the outrages which it there committed, stirred up the whole kingdom against him. In vain he asserted his innocence to the Bohemian Estates; they would not believe his protestations; vainly did he attempt to restrain the violence of his soldiery; they disregarded his orders. Persuaded that the Emperor's object was to annul the Letter of Majesty, the Protectors of Liberty armed the whole of Protestant Bohemia, and invited Matthias into the country. After the dispersion of the force he had collected at Passau, the Emperor remained helpless at Prague, where he was kept shut up like a prisoner in his palace, and separated from all his councillors. In the meantime, Matthias entered Prague amidst universal rejoicings, where Rodolph was soon afterwards weak enough to acknowledge him King of Bohemia. So hard a fate befell this Emperor; he was compelled, during his life, to abdicate in favour of his enemy that very throne, of which he had been endeavouring to deprive him after his own death. To complete his degradation, he was obliged, by a personal act of renunciation, to release his subjects in Bohemia, Silesia, and Lusatia from their allegiance, and he did it with a broken heart. All, even those he thought he had most attached to his person, had abandoned him. When he had signed the instrument, he threw his hat upon the ground, and gnawed the pen which had rendered so shameful a service.

While Rodolph thus lost one hereditary dominion after another, the imperial dignity was not much better maintained by him. Each of the religious parties into which Germany was divided, continued its efforts to advance itself at the expense of the other, or to guard against its attacks. The weaker the hand that held the sceptre, and the more the Protestants and Roman Catholics felt they were left to themselves, the more vigilant necessarily became their watchfulness, and the greater their distrust of each other. It was enough that the Emperor was ruled by Jesuits, and was guided by Spanish counsels, to excite the apprehension of the Protestants, and to afford a pretext for hostility. The rash zeal of the Jesuits, which in the pulpit and by the press disputed the validity of the religious peace, increased this distrust, and caused their adversaries to see a dangerous design in the most indifferent measures of the Roman Catholics. Every step taken in the hereditary dominions of the Emperor, for the repression of the reformed religion, was sure to draw the attention of all the Protestants of Germany; and this powerful support which the reformed subjects of Austria met, or expected to meet with from their religious confederates in the rest of Germany, was no small cause of their confidence, and of the rapid success of Matthias. It was the general belief of the Empire, that they owed the long enjoyment of the religious peace merely to the difficulties in which the Emperor was placed by the internal troubles in his dominions, and consequently they were in no haste to relieve him from them.

Almost all the affairs of the Diet were neglected, either through the procrastination of the Emperor, or through the fault of the Protestant Estates, who had determined to make no provision for the common wants of the Empire till their own grievances were removed. These grievances related principally to the misgovernment of the Emperor; the violation of the religious treaty, and the presumptuous usurpations of the Aulic Council, which in the present reign had begun to extend its jurisdiction at the expense of the Imperial Chamber. Formerly, in all disputes between the Estates, which could not be settled by club law, the Emperors had in the last resort decided of themselves, if the case were trifling, and in conjunction with the princes, if it were important; or they determined them by the advice of imperial judges who followed the court. This superior jurisdiction they had, in the end of the fifteenth century, assigned to a regular and permanent tribunal, the Imperial Chamber of Spires, in which the Estates of the Empire, that they might not be oppressed by the arbitrary appointment of the Emperor, had reserved to themselves the right of electing the assessors, and of periodically reviewing its decrees. By the religious peace, these rights of the Estates, (called the rights of presentation and visitation,) were extended also to the Lutherans, so that Protestant judges had a voice in Protestant causes, and a seeming equality obtained for both religions in this supreme tribunal.

But the enemies of the Reformation and of the freedom of the Estates, vigilant to take advantage of every incident that favoured their views, soon found means to neutralize the beneficial effects of this institution. A supreme jurisdiction over the Imperial States was gradually and skilfully usurped by a private imperial tribunal, the Aulic Council in Vienna, a court at first intended merely to advise the Emperor in the exercise of his undoubted, imperial, and personal prerogatives; a court, whose members being appointed and paid by him, had no law but the interest of their master, and no standard of equity but the advancement of the unreformed religion of which they were partisans. Before the Aulic Council were now brought several suits originating between Estates differing in religion, and which, therefore, properly belonged to the Imperial Chamber. It was not surprising if the decrees of this tribunal bore traces of their origin; if the interests of the Roman Church and of the Emperor were preferred to justice by Roman Catholic judges, and the creatures of the Emperor. Although all the Estates of Germany seemed to have equal cause for resisting so perilous an abuse, the Protestants alone, who most sensibly felt it, and even these not all at once and in a body, came forward as the defenders of German liberty, which the establishment of so arbitrary a tribunal had outraged in its most sacred point, the administration of justice. In fact, Germany would have had little cause to congratulate itself upon the abolition of club-law, and in the institution of the Imperial Chamber, if an arbitrary tribunal of the Emperor was allowed to interfere with the latter. The Estates of the German Empire would indeed have improved little upon the days of barbarism, if the Chamber of Justice in which they sat along with the Emperor as judges, and for which they had abandoned their original princely prerogative, should cease to be a court of the last resort. But the strangest contradictions were at this date to be found in the minds of men. The name of Emperor, a remnant of Roman despotism, was still associated with an idea of autocracy, which, though it formed a ridiculous inconsistency with the privileges of the Estates, was nevertheless argued for by jurists, diffused by the partisans of despotism, and believed by the ignorant.

To these general grievances was gradually added a chain of singular incidents, which at length converted the anxiety of the Protestants into utter distrust. During the Spanish persecutions in the Netherlands, several Protestant families had taken refuge in Aix-la-Chapelle, an imperial city, and attached to the Roman Catholic faith, where they settled and insensibly extended their adherents. Having succeeded by stratagem in introducing some of their members into the municipal council, they demanded a church and the public exercise of their worship, and the demand being unfavourably received, they succeeded by violence in enforcing it, and also in usurping the entire government of the city. To see so important a city in Protestant hands was too heavy a blow for the Emperor and the Roman Catholics. After all the

Emperor's requests and commands for the restoration of the olden government had proved ineffectual, the Aulic Council proclaimed the city under the ban of the Empire, which, however, was not put in force till the following reign.

Of yet greater importance were two other attempts of the Protestants to extend their influence and their power. The Elector Gebhard, of Cologne, (born Truchsess—[Grand-master of the kitchen.]—of Waldburg,) conceived for the young Countess Agnes, of Mansfield, Canoness of Gerresheim, a passion which was not unreturned. As the eyes of all Germany were directed to this intercourse, the brothers of the Countess, two zealous Calvinists, demanded satisfaction for the injured honour of their house, which, as long as the elector remained a Roman Catholic prelate, could not be repaired by marriage. They threatened the elector they would wash out this stain in his blood and their sister's, unless he either abandoned all further connexion with the countess, or consented to re-establish her reputation at the altar. The elector, indifferent to all the consequences of this step, listened to nothing but the voice of love. Whether it was in consequence of his previous inclination to the reformed doctrines, or that the charms of his mistress alone effected this wonder, he renounced the Roman Catholic faith, and led the beautiful Agnes to the altar.

This event was of the greatest importance. By the letter of the clause reserving the ecclesiastical states from the general operation of the religious peace, the elector had, by his apostacy, forfeited all right to the temporalities of his bishopric; and if, in any case, it was important for the Catholics to enforce the clause, it was so especially in the case of electorates. On the other hand, the relinquishment of so high a dignity was a severe sacrifice, and peculiarly so in the case of a tender husband, who had wished to enhance the value of his heart and hand by the gift of a principality. Moreover, the Reservatum Ecclesiasticum was a disputed article of the treaty of Augsburg; and all the German Protestants were aware of the extreme importance of wresting this fourth electorate from the opponents of their faith.—[Saxony, Brandenburg, and the Palatinate were already Protestant.]—The example had already been set in several of the ecclesiastical benefices of Lower Germany, and attended with success. Several canons of Cologne had also already embraced the Protestant confession, and were on the elector's side, while, in the city itself, he could depend upon the support of a numerous Protestant party. All these considerations, greatly strengthened by the persuasions of his friends and relations, and the promises of several German courts, determined the elector to retain his dominions, while he changed his religion.

But it was soon apparent that he had entered upon a contest which he could not carry through. Even the free toleration of the Protestant service within the territories of Cologne, had already occasioned a violent opposition on the part of the canons and Roman Catholic `Estates' of that province. The intervention of the Emperor, and a papal ban from Rome, which anathematized the elector as an apostate, and deprived him of all his dignities, temporal and spiritual, armed his own subjects and chapter against him. The Elector assembled a military force; the chapter did the same. To ensure also the aid of a strong arm, they proceeded forthwith to a new election, and chose the Bishop of Liege, a prince of Bavaria.

A civil war now commenced, which, from the strong interest which both religious parties in Germany necessarily felt in the conjuncture, was likely to terminate in a general breaking up of the religious peace. What most made the Protestants indignant, was that the Pope should have presumed, by a pretended apostolic power, to deprive a prince of the empire of his imperial dignities. Even in the golden days of their spiritual domination, this prerogative of the Pope had been disputed; how much more likely was it to be questioned at a period when his authority was entirely disowned by one party, while even with the other it rested on a tottering foundation. All the Protestant princes took up the affair warmly against the Emperor; and Henry IV. of France, then King of Navarre, left no means of negotiation untried to urge the German princes to the vigorous assertion of their rights. The issue would decide for ever the liberties of Germany. Four Protestant against three Roman Catholic voices in the Electoral College must at once have given the preponderance to the former, and for ever excluded the House of Austria from the imperial throne.

But the Elector Gebhard had embraced the Calvinist, not the Lutheran religion; and this circumstance alone was his ruin. The mutual rancour of these two churches would not permit the Lutheran Estates to regard the Elector as one of their party, and as such to lend him their effectual support. All indeed had encouraged, and promised him assistance; but only one appanaged prince of the Palatine House, the Palsgrave John Casimir, a zealous Calvinist, kept his word. Despite of the imperial prohibition, he hastened with his little army into the territories of Cologne; but without being able to effect any thing, because the Elector, who was destitute even of the first necessaries, left him totally without help. So much the more rapid was the progress of the newly-chosen elector, whom his Bavarian relations and the Spaniards from the Netherlands supported with the utmost vigour. The troops of Gebhard, left by their master without pay, abandoned one place after another to the enemy; by whom others were compelled to surrender. In his Westphalian territories, Gebhard held out for some time longer, till here, too, he was at last obliged to yield to superior force. After several vain attempts in Holland and England to obtain means for his restoration, he retired into the Chapter of Strasburg, and died dean of that cathedral; the first sacrifice to the Ecclesiastical Reservation, or rather to the want of harmony among the German Protestants.

To this dispute in Cologne was soon added another in Strasburg. Several Protestant canons of Cologne, who had been included in the same papal ban with the elector, had taken refuge within this bishopric, where they likewise held prebends. As the Roman Catholic canons of Strasburg hesitated to allow them, as being under the ban, the enjoyment of their prebends, they took violent possession of their benefices, and the support of a powerful Protestant party among the citizens soon gave them the preponderance in the chapter. The other canons thereupon retired to Alsace-Saverne, where, under the protection of the bishop, they established themselves as the only lawful chapter, and denounced that which remained in Strasburg as illegal. The latter, in the meantime, had so strengthened themselves by the reception of several Protestant colleagues of high rank, that they could venture, upon the death of the bishop, to nominate a new Protestant bishop in the person of John George of Brandenburg. The Roman Catholic canons, far from allowing this election, nominated the Bishop of Metz, a prince of Lorraine, to that dignity, who announced his promotion by immediately commencing hostilities against the territories of Strasburg.

That city now took up arms in defence of its Protestant chapter and the Prince of Brandenburg, while the other party, with the assistance of the troops of Lorraine, endeavoured to possess themselves of the temporalities of the chapter. A tedious war was the consequence, which, according to the spirit of the times, was attended with barbarous devastations. In vain did the Emperor interpose with his supreme authority to terminate the dispute; the ecclesiastical property remained for a long time divided between the two parties, till at last the Protestant prince, for a moderate pecuniary equivalent, renounced his claims; and thus, in this dispute also, the Roman Church came off victorious.

An occurrence which, soon after the adjustment of this dispute, took place in Donauwerth, a free city of Suabia, was still more critical for the whole of Protestant Germany. In this once Roman Catholic city, the Protestants, during the reigns of Ferdinand and his son, had, in the usual way, become so completely predominant, that the Roman Catholics were obliged to content themselves with a church in the Monastery of the Holy Cross, and for fear of offending the Protestants, were even forced to suppress the greater part of their religious rites. At length a fanatical abbot of this monastery ventured to defy the popular prejudices, and to arrange a public procession, preceded by the cross and banners flying; but he was soon compelled to desist from the attempt. When, a year afterwards, encouraged by a favourable imperial proclamation, the same abbot attempted to renew this procession, the citizens proceeded to open violence. The inhabitants shut the gates against the monks on their return, trampled their colours under foot, and followed them home with clamour and abuse. An imperial citation was the consequence of this act of violence; and as the exasperated populace even threatened to assault the imperial commissaries, and all attempts at an amicable adjustment were frustrated by the fanaticism of the multitude, the city was at last formally placed under the ban of the Empire, the execution of which was intrusted to Maximilian, Duke of Bavaria. The citizens, formerly so insolent, were seized with terror at the approach of the Bavarian army; pusillanimity now possessed them, though once so full of defiance, and they laid down their arms without striking a blow. The total abolition of the Protestant religion within the walls of the city was the punishment of their rebellion; it was deprived of its privileges, and, from a free city of Suabia, converted into a municipal town of Bavaria.

Two circumstances connected with this proceeding must have strongly excited the attention of the Protestants, even if the interests of religion had been less powerful on their minds. First of all, the sentence had been pronounced by the Aulic Council, an arbitrary and exclusively Roman Catholic tribunal, whose jurisdiction besides had been so warmly disputed by them; and secondly, its execution had been intrusted to the Duke of Bavaria, the head of another circle. These unconstitutional steps seemed to be the harbingers of further violent measures on the Roman Catholic side, the result, probably, of secret conferences and dangerous designs, which might perhaps end in the entire subversion of their religious liberty.

In circumstances where the law of force prevails, and security depends upon power alone, the weakest party is naturally the most busy to place itself in a posture of defence. This was now the case in Germany. If the Roman Catholics really meditated any evil against the Protestants in Germany, the probability was that the blow would fall on the south rather than the north, because, in Lower Germany, the Protestants were connected together through a long unbroken tract of country, and could therefore easily combine for their mutual support; while those in the south, detached from each other, and surrounded on all sides by Roman Catholic states, were exposed to every inroad. If, moreover, as was to be expected, the Catholics availed themselves of the divisions amongst the Protestants, and levelled their attack against one of the religious parties, it was the Calvinists who, as the weaker, and as being besides excluded from the religious treaty, were apparently in the greatest danger, and upon them would probably fall the first attack.

Both these circumstances took place in the dominions of the Elector Palatine, which possessed, in the Duke of Bavaria, a formidable neighbour, and which, by reason of their defection to Calvinism, received no protection from the Religious Peace, and had little hope of succour from the Lutheran states. No country in Germany had experienced so many revolutions in religion in so short a time as the Palatinate. In the space of sixty years this country, an unfortunate toy in the hands of its rulers, had twice adopted the doctrines of Luther, and twice relinquished them for Calvinism. The Elector Frederick III. first abandoned the confession of Augsburg, which his eldest son and successor, Lewis, immediately re-established. The Calvinists throughout the whole country were deprived of their churches, their preachers and even their teachers banished beyond the frontiers; while the prince, in his Lutheran zeal, persecuted them even in his will, by appointing none but strict and orthodox Lutherans as the guardians of his son, a minor. But this illegal testament was disregarded by his brother the Count Palatine, John Casimir, who, by the regulations of the Golden Bull, assumed the guardianship and administration of the state. Calvinistic teachers were given to the Elector Frederick IV., then only nine years of age, who were ordered, if necessary, to drive the Lutheran heresy out of the soul of their pupil with blows. If such was the treatment of the sovereign, that of the subjects may be easily conceived.

It was under this Frederick that the Palatine Court exerted itself so vigorously to unite the Protestant states of Germany in joint measures against the House of Austria, and, if possible, bring about the formation of a general confederacy. Besides that this court had always been guided by the counsels of France, with whom hatred of the House of Austria was the ruling principle, a regard for his own safety urged him to secure in time the doubtful assistance of the Lutherans against a near and overwhelming enemy. Great difficulties, however, opposed this union, because the Lutherans' dislike of the Reformed was scarcely less than the common aversion of both to the Romanists. An attempt was first made to reconcile the two professions, in order to facilitate a political union; but all these attempts failed, and generally ended in both parties adhering the more strongly to their respective opinions. Nothing then remained but to increase the fear and the distrust of the Evangelicals, and in this way to impress upon them the necessity of this alliance. The power of the Roman Catholics and the magnitude of the danger were exaggerated, accidental incidents were ascribed to deliberate plans, innocent actions misrepresented by invidious constructions, and the whole conduct of the professors of the olden religion was interpreted as the result of a well-weighed and systematic plan, which, in all probability, they were very far from having concerted.

The Diet of Ratisbon, to which the Protestants had looked forward with the hope of obtaining a renewal of the Religious Peace, had broken up without coming to a decision, and to the former grievances of the Protestant party was now added the late oppression of Donauwerth. With incredible speed, the union, so long attempted, was now brought to bear. A conference took place at Anhausen, in Franconia, at which were present the Elector Frederick

IV., from the Palatinate, the Palsgrave of Neuburg, two Margraves of Brandenburg, the Margrave of Baden, and the Duke John Frederick of Wirtemburg,—Lutherans as well as Calvinists,— who for themselves and their heirs entered into a close confederacy under the title of the Evangelical Union. The purport of this union was, that the allied princes should, in all matters relating to religion and their civil rights, support each other with arms and counsel against every aggressor, and should all stand as one man; that in case any member of the alliance should be attacked, he should be assisted by the rest with an armed force; that, if necessary, the territories, towns, and castles of the allied states should be open to his troops; and that, whatever conquests were made, should be divided among all the confederates, in proportion to the contingent furnished by each.

The direction of the whole confederacy in time of peace was conferred upon the Elector Palatine, but with a limited power. To meet the necessary expenses, subsidies were demanded, and a common fund established. Differences of religion (betwixt the Lutherans and the Calvinists) were to have no effect on this alliance, which was to subsist for ten years, every member of the union engaged at the same time to procure new members to it. The Electorate of Brandenburg adopted the alliance, that of Saxony rejected it. Hesse-Cashel could not be prevailed upon to declare itself, the Dukes of Brunswick and Luneburg also hesitated. But the three cities of the Empire, Strasburg, Nuremburg, and Ulm, were no unimportant acquisition for the league, which was in great want of their money, while their example, besides, might be followed by other imperial cities.

After the formation of this alliance, the confederate states, dispirited, and singly, little feared, adopted a bolder language. Through Prince Christian of Anhalt, they laid their common grievances and demands before the Emperor; among which the principal were the restoration of Donauwerth, the abolition of the Imperial Court, the reformation of the Emperor's own administration and that of his counsellors. For these remonstrances, they chose the moment when the Emperor had scarcely recovered breath from the troubles in his hereditary dominions,—when he had lost Hungary and Austria to Matthias, and had barely preserved his Bohemian throne by the concession of the Letter of Majesty, and finally, when through the succession of Juliers he was already threatened with the distant prospect of a new war. No wonder, then, that this dilatory prince was more irresolute than ever in his decision, and that the confederates took up arms before he could bethink himself.

The Roman Catholics regarded this confederacy with a jealous eye; the Union viewed them and the Emperor with the like distrust; the Emperor was equally suspicious of both; and thus, on all sides, alarm and animosity had reached their climax. And, as if to crown the whole, at this critical conjuncture by the death of the Duke John William of Juliers, a highly disputable succession became vacant in the territories of Juliers and Cleves.

Eight competitors laid claim to this territory, the indivisibility of which had been guaranteed by solemn treaties; and the Emperor, who seemed disposed to enter upon it as a vacant fief, might be considered as the ninth. Four of these, the Elector of Brandenburg, the Count Palatine of Neuburg, the Count Palatine of Deux Ponts, and the Margrave of Burgau, an Austrian prince, claimed it as a female fief in name of four princesses, sisters of the late duke. Two others, the Elector of Saxony, of the line of Albert, and the Duke of Saxony, of the line of Ernest, laid claim to it under a prior right of reversion granted to them by the Emperor Frederick III., and confirmed to both Saxon houses by Maximilian I. The pretensions of some foreign princes were little regarded. The best right was perhaps on the side of Brandenburg and Neuburg, and between the claims of these two it was not easy to decide. Both courts, as soon as the succession was vacant, proceeded to take possession; Brandenburg beginning, and Neuburg following the example. Both commenced their dispute with the pen, and would probably have ended it with the sword; but the interference of the Emperor, by proceeding to bring the cause before his own cognizance, and, during the progress of the suit, sequestrating the disputed countries, soon brought the contending parties to an agreement, in order to avert the common danger. They agreed to govern the duchy conjointly. In vain did the Emperor prohibit the Estates from doing homage to their new masters; in vain did he send his own relation, the Archduke Leopold, Bishop of Passau and Strasburg, into the territory of Juliers, in order, by his presence, to strengthen the imperial party. The whole country, with the exception of Juliers itself, had submitted to the Protestant princes, and in that capital the imperialists were besieged.

The dispute about the succession of Juliers was an important one to the whole German empire, and also attracted the attention of several European courts. It was not so much the question, who was or was not to possess the Duchy of Juliers;—the real question was, which of the two religious parties in Germany, the Roman Catholic or the Protestant, was to be strengthened by so important an accession—for which of the two RELIGIONS this territory was to be lost or won. The question in short was, whether Austria was to be allowed to persevere in her usurpations, and to gratify her lust of dominion by another robbery; or whether the liberties of Germany, and the balance of power, were to be maintained against her encroachments. The disputed succession of Juliers, therefore, was matter which interested all who were favourable to liberty, and hostile to Austria. The Evangelical Union, Holland, England, and particularly Henry IV. of France, were drawn into the strife.

This monarch, the flower of whose life had been spent in opposing the House of Austria and Spain, and by persevering heroism alone had surmounted the obstacles which this house had thrown between him and the French throne, had been no idle spectator of the troubles in Germany. This contest of the Estates with the Emperor was the means of giving and securing peace to France. The Protestants and the Turks were the two salutary weights which kept down the Austrian power in the East and West; but it would rise again in all its terrors, if once it were allowed to remove this pressure. Henry the Fourth had before his eyes for half a lifetime, the uninterrupted spectacle of Austrian ambition and Austrian lust of dominion, which neither adversity nor poverty of talents, though generally they check all human passions, could extinguish in a bosom wherein flowed one drop of the blood of Ferdinand of Arragon. Austrian ambition had destroyed for a century the peace of Europe, and effected the most violent changes in the heart of its most considerable states. It had deprived the fields of husbandmen, the workshops of artisans, to fill the land with enormous armies, and to cover the commercial sea with hostile fleets. It had imposed upon the princes of Europe the necessity of fettering the industry of their subjects by unheard-of imposts; and of wasting in self-defence the best strength of their states, which was thus lost to the prosperity of their inhabitants. For Europe there was no peace, for its states no welfare, for the people's happiness no security or permanence, so long as this dangerous house was permitted to disturb at pleasure the repose of the world.

Such considerations clouded the mind of Henry at the close of his glorious career. What had it not cost him to reduce to order the troubled chaos into which France had been plunged by the tumult of civil war, fomented and supported by this very Austria! Every great mind labours for eternity; and what security had Henry for the endurance of that prosperity which he had gained for France, so long as Austria and Spain formed a single power, which did indeed lie exhausted for the present, but which required only one lucky chance to be speedily re-united, and to spring up again as formidable as ever. If he would bequeath to his successors a firmly established throne, and a durable prosperity to his subjects, this dangerous power must be for ever disarmed. This was the source of that irreconcileable enmity which Henry had sworn to the House of Austria, a hatred unextinguishable, ardent, and well-founded as that of Hannibal against the people of Romulus, but ennobled by a purer origin.

The other European powers had the same inducements to action as Henry, but all of them had not that enlightened policy, nor that disinterested courage to act upon the impulse. All men, without distinction, are allured by immediate advantages; great minds alone are excited by distant good. So long as wisdom in its projects calculates upon wisdom, or relies upon its own strength, it forms none but chimerical schemes, and runs a risk of making itself the laughter of the world; but it is certain of success, and may reckon upon aid and admiration when it finds a place in its intellectual plans for barbarism, rapacity, and superstition, and can render the selfish passions of mankind the executors of its purposes.

In the first point of view, Henry's well-known project of expelling the House of Austria from all its possessions, and dividing the spoil among the European powers, deserves the title of a chimera, which men have so liberally bestowed upon it; but did it merit that appellation in the second? It had never entered into the head of that excellent monarch, in the choice of those who must be the instruments of his designs, to reckon on the sufficiency of such motives as animated himself and Sully to the enterprise. All the states whose co-operation was necessary, were to be persuaded to the work by the strongest motives that can set a political power in action. From the Protestants in Germany nothing more was required than that which, on other grounds, had been long their object,—their throwing off the Austrian yoke; from the Flemings, a similar revolt from the Spaniards. To the Pope and all the Italian republics no inducement could be more powerful than the hope of driving the Spaniards for ever from their peninsula; for England, nothing more desirable than a revolution which should free it from its bitterest enemy. By this division of the Austrian conquests, every power gained either land or freedom, new possessions or security for the old; and as all gained, the balance of power remained undisturbed. France might magnanimously decline a share in the spoil, because by the ruin of Austria it doubly profited, and was most powerful if it did not become more powerful. Finally, upon condition of ridding Europe of their presence, the posterity of Hapsburg were to be allowed the liberty of augmenting her territories in all the other known or yet undiscovered portions of the globe. But the dagger of Ravaillac delivered Austria from her danger, to postpone for some centuries longer the tranquillity of Europe.

With his view directed to this project, Henry felt the necessity of taking a prompt and active part in the important events of the Evangelical Union, and the disputed succession of Juliers. His emissaries were busy in all the courts of Germany, and the little which they published or allowed to escape of the great political secrets of their master, was sufficient to win over minds inflamed by so ardent a hatred to Austria, and by so strong a desire of aggrandizement. The prudent policy of Henry cemented the Union still more closely, and the powerful aid which he bound himself to furnish, raised the courage of the confederates into the firmest confidence. A numerous French army, led by the king in person, was to meet the troops of the Union on the banks of the Rhine, and to assist in effecting the conquest of Juliers and Cleves; then, in conjunction with the Germans, it was to march into Italy, (where Savoy, Venice, and the Pope were even now ready with a powerful reinforcement,) and to overthrow the Spanish dominion in that quarter. This victorious army was then to penetrate by Lombardy into the hereditary dominions of Hapsburg; and there, favoured by a general insurrection of the Protestants, destroy the power of Austria in all its German territories, in Bohemia, Hungary, and Transylvania. The Brabanters and Hollanders, supported by French auxiliaries, would in the meantime shake off the Spanish tyranny in the Netherlands; and thus the mighty stream which, only a short time before, had so fearfully overflowed its banks, threatening to overwhelm in its troubled waters the liberties of Europe, would then roll silent and forgotten behind the Pyrenean mountains.

At other times, the French had boasted of their rapidity of action, but upon this occasion they were outstripped by the Germans. An army of the confederates entered Alsace before Henry made his appearance there, and an Austrian army, which the Bishop of Strasburg and Passau had assembled in that quarter for an expedition against Juliers, was dispersed. Henry IV. had formed his plan as a statesman and a king, but he had intrusted its execution to plunderers. According to his design, no Roman Catholic state was to have cause to think this preparation aimed against itself, or to make the quarrel of Austria its own. Religion was in nowise to be mixed up with the matter. But how could the German princes forget their own purposes in furthering the plans of Henry? Actuated as they were by the desire of aggrandizement and by religious hatred, was it to be supposed that they would not gratify, in every passing opportunity, their ruling passions to the utmost? Like vultures, they stooped upon the territories of the ecclesiastical princes, and always chose those rich countries for their quarters, though to reach them they must make ever so wide a detour from their direct route. They levied contributions as in an enemy's country, seized upon the revenues, and exacted, by violence, what they could not obtain of free-will. Not to leave the Roman Catholics in doubt as to the true objects of their expedition, they announced, openly and intelligibly enough, the fate that awaited the property of the church. So little had Henry IV. and the German princes understood each other in their plan of operations, so much had the excellent king been mistaken in his instruments. It is an unfailing maxim, that, if policy enjoins an act of violence, its execution ought never to be entrusted to the violent; and that he only ought to be trusted with the violation of order by whom order is held sacred.

Both the past conduct of the Union, which was condemned even by several of the evangelical states, and the apprehension of even worse treatment, aroused the Roman Catholics to something beyond mere inactive indignation. As to the Emperor, his authority had sunk too low to afford them any security against such an enemy. It was their Union that rendered the confederates so formidable and so insolent; and another union must now be opposed to them.

The Bishop of Wurtzburg formed the plan of the Catholic union, which was distinguished from the evangelical by the title of the League. The objects agreed upon were nearly the same as those which constituted the groundwork of the Union. Bishops formed its principal members, and at its head was placed Maximilian, Duke of Bavaria. As the only influential secular member of the confederacy, he was entrusted with far more extensive powers than the Protestants had committed to their chief. In addition to the duke's being the sole head of the League's military power, whereby their operations acquired a speed and weight unattainable by the Union, they had also the advantage that supplies flowed in much more regularly from the rich prelates, than the latter could obtain them from the poor evangelical states. Without offering to the Emperor, as the sovereign of a Roman Catholic state, any share in their confederacy, without even communicating its existence to him as emperor, the League arose at once formidable and threatening; with strength sufficient to crush the Protestant Union and to maintain itself under three emperors. It contended, indeed, for Austria, in so far as it fought against the Protestant princes; but Austria herself had soon cause to tremble before it.

The arms of the Union had, in the meantime, been tolerably successful in Juliers and in Alsace; Juliers was closely blockaded, and the whole bishopric of Strasburg was in their power. But here their splendid achievements came to an end. No French army appeared upon the Rhine; for he who was to be its leader, he who was the animating soul of the whole enterprize, Henry IV., was no more! Their supplies were on the wane; the Estates refused to grant new subsidies; and the confederate free cities were offended that their money should be liberally, but their advice so sparingly called for. Especially were they displeased at being put to expense for the expedition against Juliers, which had been expressly excluded from the affairs of the Union—at the united princes appropriating to themselves large pensions out of the common treasure—and, above all, at their refusing to give any account of its expenditure.

The Union was thus verging to its fall, at the moment when the League started to oppose it in the vigour of its strength. Want of supplies disabled the confederates from any longer keeping the field. And yet it was dangerous to lay down their weapons in the sight of an armed enemy. To secure themselves at least on one side, they hastened to conclude a peace with their old enemy, the Archduke Leopold; and both parties agreed to withdraw their troops from Alsace, to exchange prisoners, and to bury all that had been done in oblivion. Thus ended in nothing all these promising preparations.

The same imperious tone with which the Union, in the confidence of its strength, had menaced the Roman Catholics of Germany, was now retorted by the League upon themselves and their troops. The traces of their march were pointed out to them, and plainly branded with the hard epithets they had deserved. The chapters of Wurtzburg, Bamberg, Strasburg, Mentz, Treves, Cologne, and several others, had experienced their destructive presence; to all these the damage done was to be made good, the free passage by land and by water restored, (for the Protestants had even seized on the navigation of the Rhine,) and everything replaced on its former footing. Above all, the parties to the Union were called on to declare expressly and unequivocally its intentions. It was now their turn to yield to superior strength. They had not calculated on so formidable an opponent; but they themselves had taught the Roman Catholics the secret of their strength. It was humiliating to their pride to sue for peace, but they might think themselves fortunate in obtaining it. The one party promised restitution, the other forgiveness. All laid down their arms. The storm of war once more rolled by, and a temporary calm succeeded. The insurrection in Bohemia then broke out, which deprived the Emperor of the last of his hereditary dominions, but in this dispute neither the Union nor the League took any share.

At length the Emperor died in 1612, as little regretted in his coffin as noticed on the throne. Long afterwards, when the miseries of succeeding reigns had made the misfortunes of his reign forgotten, a halo spread about his memory, and so fearful a night set in upon Germany, that, with tears of blood, people prayed for the return of such an emperor.

Rodolph never could be prevailed upon to choose a successor in the empire, and all awaited with anxiety the approaching vacancy of the throne; but, beyond all hope, Matthias at once ascended it, and without opposition. The Roman Catholics gave him their voices, because they hoped the best from his vigour and activity; the Protestants gave him theirs, because they hoped every thing from his weakness. It is not difficult to reconcile this contradiction. The one relied on what he had once appeared; the other judged him by what he seemed at present.

The moment of a new accession is always a day of hope; and the first Diet of a king in elective monarchies is usually his severest trial. Every old grievance is brought forward, and new ones are sought out, that they may be included in the expected reform; quite a new world is expected to commence with the new reign. The important services which, in his insurrection, their religious confederates in Austria had rendered to Matthias, were still fresh in the minds of the Protestant free cities, and, above all, the price which they had exacted for their services seemed now to serve them also as a model.

It was by the favour of the Protestant Estates in Austria and Moravia that Matthias had sought and really found the way to his brother's throne; but, hurried on by his ambitious views, he never reflected that a way was thus opened for the States to give laws to their sovereign. This discovery soon awoke him from the intoxication of success. Scarcely had he shown himself in triumph to his Austrian subjects, after his victorious expedition to Bohemia, when a humble petition awaited him which was quite sufficient to poison his whole triumph. They required, before doing homage, unlimited religious toleration in the cities and market towns, perfect equality of rights between Roman Catholics and Protestants, and a full and equal admissibility of the latter to all offices of state. In several places, they of themselves assumed these privileges, and, reckoning on a change of administration, restored the Protestant religion where the late Emperor had suppressed it. Matthias, it is true, had not scrupled to make use of the grievances of the Protestants for his own ends against the Emperor; but it was far from being his intention to relieve them. By a firm and resolute tone he hoped to check, at once, these presumptuous demands. He spoke of his hereditary title to these territories, and would hear of no stipulations before the act of homage. A like unconditional submission had been rendered by their neighbours, the inhabitants of Styria, to the Archduke Ferdinand, who, however, had soon reason to repent of it. Warned by this example, the Austrian States persisted in their refusal; and, to avoid being compelled by force to do homage, their deputies (after urging their Roman Catholic colleagues to a similar resistance) immediately left the capital, and began to levy troops.

They took steps to renew their old alliance with Hungary, drew the Protestant princes into their interests, and set themselves seriously to work to accomplish their object by force of arms.

With the more exorbitant demands of the Hungarians Matthias had not hesitated to comply. For Hungary was an elective monarchy, and the republican constitution of the country justified to himself their demands, and to the Roman Catholic world his concessions. In Austria, on the contrary, his predecessors had exercised far higher prerogatives, which he could not relinquish at the demand of the Estates without incurring the scorn of Roman Catholic Europe, the enmity of Spain and Rome, and the contempt of his own Roman Catholic subjects. His exclusively Romish council, among which the Bishop of Vienna, Melchio Kiesel, had the chief influence, exhorted him to see all the churches extorted from him by the Protestants, rather than to concede one to them as a matter of right.

But by ill luck this difficulty occurred at a time when the Emperor Rodolph was yet alive, and a spectator of this scene, and who might easily have been tempted to employ against his brother the same weapons which the latter had successfully directed against him—namely, an understanding with his rebellious subjects. To avoid this blow, Matthias willingly availed himself of the offer made by Moravia, to act as mediator between him and the Estates of Austria. Representatives of both parties met in Vienna, when the Austrian deputies held language which would have excited surprise even in the English Parliament. "The Protestants," they said, "are determined to be not worse treated in their native country than the handful of Romanists. By the help of his Protestant nobles had Matthias reduced the Emperor to submission; where 80 Papists were to be found, 300 Protestant barons might be counted. The example of Rodolph should be a warning to Matthias. He should take care that he did not lose the terrestrial, in attempting to make conquests for the celestial." As the Moravian States, instead of using their powers as mediators for the Emperor's advantage, finally adopted the cause of their co-religionists of Austria; as the Union in Germany came forward to afford them its most active support, and as Matthias dreaded reprisals on the part of the Emperor, he was at length compelled to make the desired declaration in favour of the Evangelical Church.

This behaviour of the Austrian Estates towards their Archduke was now imitated by the Protestant Estates of the Empire towards their Emperor, and they promised themselves the same favourable results. At his first Diet at Ratisbon in 1613, when the most pressing affairs were waiting for decision—when a general contribution was indispensable for a war against Turkey, and against Bethlem Gabor in Transylvania, who by Turkish aid had forcibly usurped the sovereignty of that land, and even threatened Hungary—they surprised him with an entirely new demand. The Roman Catholic votes were still the most numerous in the Diet; and as every thing was decided by a plurality of voices, the Protestant party, however closely united, were entirely without consideration. The advantage of this majority the Roman Catholics were now called on to relinquish; henceforward no one religious party was to be permitted to dictate to the other by means of its invariable superiority. And in truth, if the evangelical religion was really to be represented in the Diet, it was self-evident that it must not be shut out from the possibility of making use of that privilege, merely from the constitution of the Diet itself. Complaints of the judicial usurpations of the Aulic Council, and of the oppression of the Protestants, accompanied this demand, and the deputies of the Estates were instructed to take no part in any general deliberations till a favourable answer should be given on this preliminary point.

The Diet was torn asunder by this dangerous division, which threatened to destroy for ever the unity of its deliberations. Sincerely as the Emperor might have wished, after the example of his father Maximilian, to preserve a prudent balance between the two religions, the present conduct of the Protestants seemed to leave him nothing but a critical choice between the two. In his present necessities a general contribution from the Estates was indispensable to him; and yet he could not conciliate the one party without sacrificing the support of the other. Insecure as he felt his situation to be in his own hereditary dominions, he could not but tremble at the idea, however remote, of an open war with the Protestants. But the eyes of the whole Roman Catholic world, which were attentively regarding his conduct, the remonstrances of the Roman Catholic Estates, and of the Courts of Rome and Spain, as little permitted him to favour the Protestant at the expense of the Romish religion.

So critical a situation would have paralysed a greater mind than Matthias; and his own prudence would scarcely have extricated him from his dilemma. But the interests of the Roman Catholics were closely interwoven with the imperial authority; if they suffered this to fall, the ecclesiastical princes in particular would be without a bulwark against the attacks of the Protestants. Now, then, that they saw the Emperor wavering, they thought it high time to reassure his sinking courage. They imparted to him the secret of their League, and acquainted him with its whole constitution, resources and power. Little comforting as such a revelation must have been to the Emperor, the prospect of so powerful a support gave him greater boldness to oppose the Protestants. Their demands were rejected, and the Diet broke up without coming to a decision. But Matthias was the victim of this dispute. The Protestants refused him their supplies, and made him alone suffer for the inflexibility of the Roman Catholics.

The Turks, however, appeared willing to prolong the cessation of hostilities, and Bethlem Gabor was left in peaceable possession of Transylvania. The empire was now free from foreign enemies; and even at home, in the midst of all these fearful disputes, peace still reigned. An unexpected accident had given a singular turn to the dispute as to the succession of Juliers. This duchy was still ruled conjointly by the Electoral House of Brandenburg and the Palatine of Neuburg; and a marriage between the Prince of Neuburg and a Princess of Brandenburg was to have inseparably united the interests of the two houses. But the whole scheme was upset by a box on the ear, which, in a drunken brawl, the Elector of Brandenburg unfortunately inflicted upon his intended son-in-law. From this moment the good understanding between the two houses was at an end. The Prince of Neuburg embraced popery. The hand of a princess of Bavaria rewarded his apostacy, and the strong support of Bavaria and Spain was the natural result of both. To secure to the Palatine the exclusive possession of Juliers, the Spanish troops from the Netherlands were marched into the Palatinate. To rid himself of these guests, the Elector of Brandenburg called the Flemings to his assistance, whom he sought to propitiate by embracing the Calvinist religion. Both Spanish and Dutch armies appeared, but, as it seemed, only to make conquests for themselves.

The neighbouring war of the Netherlands seemed now about to be decided on German ground; and what an inexhaustible mine of combustibles lay here ready for it! The Protestants saw with consternation the Spaniards establishing themselves upon the Lower Rhine; with still greater anxiety did the Roman Catholics see the Hollanders bursting through the frontiers of the empire. It was in the west that the mine was expected to explode which had long been dug under the whole of Germany. To the west, apprehension and anxiety turned; but the spark which kindled the flame came unexpectedly from the east.

The tranquillity which Rodolph II.'s 'Letter of Majesty' had established in Bohemia lasted for some time, under the administration of Matthias, till the nomination of a new heir to this kingdom in the person of Ferdinand of Gratz.

This prince, whom we shall afterwards become better acquainted with under the title of Ferdinand II., Emperor of Germany, had, by the violent extirpation of the Protestant religion within his hereditary dominions, announced himself as an inexorable zealot for popery, and was consequently looked upon by the Roman Catholic part of Bohemia as the future pillar of their church. The declining health of the Emperor brought on this hour rapidly; and, relying on so powerful a supporter, the Bohemian Papists began to treat the Protestants with little moderation. The Protestant vassals of Roman Catholic nobles, in particular, experienced the harshest treatment. At length several of the former were incautious enough to speak somewhat loudly of their hopes, and by threatening hints to awaken among the Protestants a suspicion of their future sovereign. But this mistrust would never have broken out into actual violence, had the Roman Catholics confined themselves to general expressions, and not by attacks on individuals furnished the discontent of the people with enterprising leaders.

Henry Matthias, Count Thurn, not a native of Bohemia, but proprietor of some estates in that kingdom, had, by his zeal for the Protestant cause, and an enthusiastic attachment to his newly adopted country, gained the entire confidence of the Utraquists, which opened him the way to the most important posts. He had fought with great glory against the Turks, and won by a flattering address the hearts of the multitude. Of a hot and impetuous disposition, which loved tumult because his talents shone in it—rash and thoughtless enough to undertake things which cold prudence and a calmer temper would not have ventured upon—unscrupulous enough, where the gratification of his passions was concerned, to sport with the fate of thousands, and at the same time politic enough to hold in leading-strings such a people as the Bohemians then were. He had already taken an active part in the troubles under Rodolph's administration; and the Letter of Majesty which the States had extorted from that Emperor, was chiefly to be laid to his merit.

The court had intrusted to him, as burgrave or castellan of Calstein, the custody of the Bohemian crown, and of the national charter. But the nation had placed in his hands something far more important—ITSELF—with the office of defender or protector of the faith. The aristocracy by which the Emperor was ruled, imprudently deprived him of this harmless guardianship of the dead, to leave him his full influence over the living. They took from him his office of burgrave, or constable of the castle, which had rendered him dependent on the court, thereby opening his eyes to the importance of the other which remained, and wounded his vanity, which yet was the thing that made his ambition harmless. From this moment he was actuated solely by a desire of revenge; and the opportunity of gratifying it was not long wanting.

In the Royal Letter which the Bohemians had extorted from Rodolph II., as well as in the German religious treaty, one material article remained undetermined. All the privileges granted by the latter to the Protestants, were conceived in favour of the Estates or governing bodies, not of the subjects; for only to those of the ecclesiastical states had a toleration, and that precarious, been conceded. The Bohemian Letter of Majesty, in the same manner, spoke only of the Estates and imperial towns, the magistrates of which had contrived to obtain equal privileges with the former. These alone were free to erect churches and schools, and openly to celebrate their Protestant worship; in all other towns, it was left entirely to the government to which they belonged, to determine the religion of the inhabitants. The Estates of the Empire had availed themselves of this privilege in its fullest extent; the secular indeed without opposition; while the ecclesiastical, in whose case the declaration of Ferdinand had limited this privilege, disputed, not without reason, the validity of that limitation. What was a disputed point in the religious treaty, was left still more doubtful in the Letter of Majesty; in the former, the construction was not doubtful, but it was a question how far obedience might be compulsory; in the latter, the interpretation was left to the states. The subjects of the ecclesiastical Estates in Bohemia thought themselves entitled to the same rights which the declaration of Ferdinand secured to the subjects of German bishops, they considered themselves on an equality with the subjects of imperial towns, because they looked upon the ecclesiastical property as part of the royal demesnes. In the little town of Klostergrab, subject to the Archbishop of Prague; and in Braunau, which belonged to the abbot of that monastery, churches were founded by the Protestants, and completed notwithstanding the opposition of their superiors, and the disapprobation of the Emperor.

In the meantime, the vigilance of the defenders had somewhat relaxed, and the court thought it might venture on a decisive step. By the Emperor's orders, the church at Klostergrab was pulled down; that at Braunau forcibly shut up, and the most turbulent of the citizens thrown into prison. A general commotion among the Protestants was the consequence of this measure; a loud outcry was everywhere raised at this violation of the Letter of Majesty; and Count Thurn, animated by revenge, and particularly called upon by his office of defender, showed himself not a little busy in inflaming the minds of the people. At his instigation deputies were summoned to Prague from every circle in the empire, to concert the necessary measures against the common danger. It was resolved to petition the Emperor to press for the liberation of the prisoners. The answer of the Emperor, already offensive to the states, from its being addressed, not to them, but to his viceroy, denounced their conduct as illegal and rebellious, justified what had been done at Klostergrab and Braunau as the result of an imperial mandate, and contained some passages that might be construed into threats.

Count Thurn did not fail to augment the unfavourable impression which this imperial edict made upon the assembled Estates. He pointed out to them the danger in which all who had signed the petition were involved, and sought by working on their resentment and fears to hurry them into violent resolutions. To have caused their immediate revolt against the Emperor, would have been, as yet, too bold a measure. It was only step by step that he would lead them on to this unavoidable result. He held it, therefore, advisable first to direct their indignation against the Emperor's counsellors; and for that purpose circulated a report, that the imperial proclamation had been drawn up by the government at Prague, and only signed in Vienna. Among the imperial delegates, the chief objects of the popular hatred, were the President of the Chamber, Slawata, and Baron Martinitz, who had been elected in place of Count Thurn, Burgrave of Calstein. Both had long before evinced pretty openly their hostile feelings towards the Protestants, by alone refusing to be present at the sitting at which the Letter of Majesty had been inserted in the Bohemian constitution. A threat was made at the time to make them responsible for every violation of the Letter of Majesty; and from this moment, whatever evil befell the Protestants was set down, and not without reason, to their account. Of all the Roman Catholic nobles, these two had treated their Protestant vassals with the greatest harshness. They were accused of hunting them with dogs to the mass, and of endeavouring to drive them to popery by a denial of the rites of baptism, marriage, and burial. Against two characters so unpopular the public indignation was easily excited, and they were marked out for a sacrifice to the general indignation.

On the 23rd of May, 1618, the deputies appeared armed, and in great numbers, at the royal palace, and forced their way into the hall where the Commissioners Sternberg, Martinitz, Lobkowitz, and Slawata were assembled. In a threatening tone they demanded to know from each of them, whether he had taken any part, or had consented to, the imperial proclamation. Sternberg received them with composure, Martinitz and Slawata with defiance. This decided their fate; Sternberg and Lobkowitz, less hated, and more feared, were led by the arm out of the room; Martinitz and Slawata were seized, dragged to a window, and precipitated from a height of eighty feet, into the castle trench. Their creature, the secretary Fabricius, was thrown after them. This singular mode of execution naturally excited the surprise of civilized nations. The Bohemians justified it as a national custom, and saw nothing remarkable in the whole affair, excepting that any one should have got up again safe and sound after such a fall. A dunghill, on which the imperial commissioners chanced to be deposited, had saved them from injury.

It was not to be expected that this summary mode of proceeding would much increase the favour of the parties with the Emperor, but this was the very position to which Count Thurn wished to bring them. If, from the fear of uncertain danger, they had permitted themselves such an act of violence, the certain expectation of punishment, and the now urgent necessity of making themselves secure, would plunge them still deeper into guilt. By this brutal act of self-redress, no room was left for irresolution or repentance, and it seemed as if a single crime could be absolved only by a series of violences. As the deed itself could not be undone, nothing was left but to disarm the hand of punishment. Thirty directors were appointed to organise a regular insurrection. They seized upon all the offices of state, and all the imperial revenues, took into their own service the royal functionaries and the soldiers, and summoned the whole Bohemian nation to avenge the common cause. The Jesuits, whom the common hatred accused as the instigators of every previous oppression, were banished the kingdom, and this harsh measure the Estates found it necessary to justify in a formal manifesto. These various steps were taken for the preservation of the royal authority and the laws—the language of all rebels till fortune has decided in their favour.

The emotion which the news of the Bohemian insurrection excited at the imperial court, was much less lively than such intelligence deserved. The Emperor Matthias was no longer the resolute spirit that formerly sought out his king and master in the very bosom of his people, and hurled him from three thrones. The confidence and courage which had animated him in an usurpation, deserted him in a legitimate self-defence. The Bohemian rebels had first taken up arms, and the nature of circumstances drove him to join them. But he could not hope to confine such a war to Bohemia. In all the territories under his dominion, the Protestants were united by a dangerous sympathy—the common danger of their religion might suddenly combine them all into a formidable republic. What could he oppose to such an enemy, if the Protestant portion of his subjects deserted him? And would not both parties exhaust themselves in so ruinous a civil war? How much was at stake if he lost; and if he won, whom else would he destroy but his own subjects?

Considerations such as these inclined the Emperor and his council to concessions and pacific measures, but it was in this very spirit of concession that, as others would have it, lay the origin of the evil. The Archduke Ferdinand of Gratz congratulated the Emperor upon an event, which would justify in the eyes of all Europe the severest measures against the Bohemian Protestants. "Disobedience, lawlessness, and insurrection," he said, "went always hand-in-hand with Protestantism. Every privilege which had been conceded to the Estates by himself and his predecessor, had had no other effect than to raise their demands. All the measures of the heretics were aimed against the imperial authority. Step by step had they advanced from defiance to defiance up to this last aggression; in a short time they would assail all that remained to be assailed, in the person of the Emperor. In arms alone was there any safety against such an enemy—peace and subordination could be only established upon the ruins of their dangerous privileges; security for the Catholic belief was to be found only in the total destruction of this sect. Uncertain, it was true, might be the event of the war, but inevitable was the ruin if it were pretermitted. The confiscation of the lands of the rebels would richly indemnify them for its expenses, while the terror of punishment would teach the other states the wisdom of a prompt obedience in future." Were the Bohemian Protestants to blame, if they armed themselves in time against the enforcement of such maxims? The insurrection in Bohemia, besides, was directed only against the successor of the Emperor, not against himself, who had done nothing to justify the alarm of the Protestants. To exclude this prince from the Bohemian throne, arms had before been taken up under Matthias, though as long as this Emperor lived, his subjects had kept within the bounds of an apparent submission.

But Bohemia was in arms, and unarmed, the Emperor dared not even offer them peace. For this purpose, Spain supplied gold, and promised to send troops from Italy and the Netherlands. Count Bucquoi, a native of the Netherlands, was named generalissimo, because no native could be trusted, and Count Dampierre, another foreigner, commanded under him. Before the army took the field, the Emperor endeavoured to bring about an amicable arrangement, by the publication of a manifesto. In this he assured the Bohemians, "that he held sacred the Letter of Majesty—that he had not formed any resolutions inimical to their religion or their privileges, and that his present preparations were forced upon him by their own. As soon as the nation laid down their arms, he also would disband his army." But this gracious letter failed of its effect, because the leaders of the insurrection contrived to hide from the people the Emperor's good intentions. Instead of this, they circulated the most alarming reports from the pulpit, and by pamphlets, and terrified the deluded populace with threatened horrors of another Saint Bartholomew's that existed only in their own imagination. All Bohemia, with the exception of three towns, Budweiss, Krummau, and Pilsen, took part in this insurrection. These three towns, inhabited principally by Roman Catholics, alone had the courage, in this general revolt, to hold out for the Emperor, who promised them assistance. But it could not escape Count Thurn, how dangerous it was to leave in hostile hands three places of such importance, which would at all times keep open for the imperial troops an entrance into the kingdom. With prompt determination he appeared before Budweiss and Krummau, in the hope of terrifying them into a surrender. Krummau surrendered, but all his attacks were steadfastly repulsed by Budweiss.

And now, too, the Emperor began to show more earnestness and energy. Bucquoi and Dampierre, with two armies, fell upon the Bohemian territories, which they treated as a hostile country. But the imperial generals found the march to Prague more difficult than they had expected. Every pass, every position that was the least tenable, must be opened by the sword, and resistance increased at each fresh step they took, for the outrages of their troops, chiefly consisting of Hungarians and Walloons, drove their friends to revolt and their enemies to despair. But even now that his troops had penetrated into Bohemia, the Emperor continued to offer the Estates peace, and to show himself ready for an amicable adjustment. But the new prospects which opened upon them, raised the courage of the revolters. Moravia espoused their party; and from Germany appeared to them a defender equally intrepid and unexpected, in the person of Count Mansfeld.

The heads of the Evangelic Union had been silent but not inactive spectators of the movements in Bohemia. Both were contending for the same cause, and against the same enemy. In the fate of the Bohemians, their confederates in the faith might read their own; and the cause of this people was represented as of solemn concern to the whole German union. True to these principles, the Unionists supported the courage of the insurgents by promises of assistance; and a fortunate accident now enabled them, beyond their hopes, to fulfil them.

The instrument by which the House of Austria was humbled in Germany, was Peter Ernest, Count Mansfeld, the son of a distinguished Austrian officer, Ernest von Mansfeld, who for some time had commanded with repute the Spanish army in the Netherlands. His first campaigns in Juliers and Alsace had been made in the service of this house, and under the banner of the Archduke Leopold, against the Protestant religion and the liberties of Germany. But insensibly won by the principles of this religion, he abandoned a leader whose selfishness denied him the reimbursement of the monies expended in his cause, and he transferred his zeal and a victorious sword to the Evangelic Union. It happened just then that the Duke of Savoy, an ally of the Union, demanded assistance in a war against Spain. They assigned to him their newly acquired servant, and Mansfeld received instructions to raise an army of 4000 men in Germany, in the cause and in the pay of the duke. The army was ready to march at the very moment when the flames of war burst out in Bohemia, and the duke, who at the time did not stand in need of its services, placed it at the disposal of the Union. Nothing could be more welcome to these troops than the prospect of aiding their confederates in Bohemia, at the cost of a third party. Mansfeld received orders forthwith to march with these 4000 men into that kingdom; and a pretended Bohemian commission was given to blind the public as to the true author of this levy.

This Mansfeld now appeared in Bohemia, and, by the occupation of Pilsen, strongly fortified and favourable to the Emperor, obtained a firm footing in the country. The courage of the rebels was farther increased by succours which the Silesian States despatched to their assistance. Between these and the Imperialists, several battles were fought, far indeed from decisive, but only on that account the more destructive, which served as the prelude to a more serious war. To check the vigour of his military operations, a negotiation was entered into with the Emperor, and a disposition was shown to accept the proffered mediation of Saxony. But before the event could prove how little sincerity there was in these proposals, the Emperor was removed from the scene by death.

What now had Matthias done to justify the expectations which he had excited by the overthrow of his predecessor? Was it worth while to ascend a brother's throne through guilt, and then maintain it with so little dignity, and leave it with so little renown? As long as Matthias sat on the throne, he had to atone for the imprudence by which he had gained it. To enjoy the regal dignity a few years sooner, he had shackled the free exercise of its prerogatives. The slender portion of independence left him by the growing power of the Estates, was still farther lessened by the encroachments of his relations. Sickly and childless he saw the attention of the world turned to an ambitious heir who was impatiently anticipating his fate; and who, by his interference with the closing administration, was already opening his own.

With Matthias, the reigning line of the German House of Austria was in a manner extinct; for of all the sons of Maximilian, one only was now alive, the weak and childless Archduke Albert, in the Netherlands, who had already renounced his claims to the inheritance in favour of the line of Gratz. The Spanish House had also, in a secret bond, resigned its pretensions to the Austrian possessions in behalf of the Archduke Ferdinand of Styria, in whom the branch of Hapsburg was about to put forth new shoots, and the former greatness of Austria to experience a revival.

The father of Ferdinand was the Archduke Charles of Carniola, Carinthia, and Styria, the youngest brother of the Emperor Maximilian II.; his mother a princess of Bavaria. Having lost his father at twelve years of age, he was intrusted by the archduchess to the guardianship of her brother William, Duke of Bavaria, under whose eyes he was instructed and educated by Jesuits at the Academy of Ingolstadt. What principles he was likely to imbibe by his intercourse with a prince, who from motives of devotion had abdicated his government, may be easily conceived. Care was taken to point out to him, on the one hand, the weak indulgence of Maximilian's house towards the adherents of the new doctrines, and the consequent troubles of their dominions; on the other, the blessings of Bavaria, and the inflexible religious zeal of its rulers; between these two examples he was left to choose for himself.

Formed in this school to be a stout champion of the faith, and a prompt instrument of the church, he left Bavaria, after a residence of five years, to assume the government of his hereditary dominions. The Estates of Carniola, Carinthia, and Styria, who, before doing homage, demanded a guarantee for freedom of religion, were told that religious liberty has nothing to do with their allegiance. The oath was put to them without conditions, and unconditionally taken. Many years, however, elapsed, ere the designs which had been planned at Ingolstadt were ripe for execution. Before attempting to carry them into effect, he sought in person at Loretto the favour of the Virgin, and received the apostolic benediction in Rome at the feet of Clement VIII.

These designs were nothing less than the expulsion of Protestantism from a country where it had the advantage of numbers, and had been legally recognized by a formal act of toleration, granted by his father to the noble and knightly estates of the land. A grant so formally ratified could not be revoked without danger; but no difficulties could deter the pious pupil of the Jesuits. The example of other states, both Roman Catholic and Protestant, which within their own territories had exercised unquestioned a right of reformation, and the abuse which the Estates of Styria made of their religious liberties, would serve as a justification of this violent procedure. Under the shelter of an absurd positive law, those of equity and prudence might, it was thought, be safely despised. In the execution of these unrighteous designs, Ferdinand did, it must be owned, display no common courage and perseverance. Without tumult, and we may add, without cruelty, he suppressed the Protestant service in one town after another, and in a few years, to the astonishment of Germany, this dangerous work was brought to a successful end.

But, while the Roman Catholics admired him as a hero, and the champion of the church, the Protestants began to combine against him as against their most dangerous enemy. And yet Matthias's intention to bequeath to him the succession, met with little or no opposition in the elective states of Austria. Even the Bohemians agreed to receive him as their future king, on very favourable conditions. It was not until afterwards, when they had experienced the pernicious influence of his councils on the administration of the Emperor, that their anxiety was first excited; and then several projects, in his handwriting, which an unlucky chance threw into their hands, as they plainly evinced his disposition towards them, carried their apprehension to the utmost pitch. In particular, they were alarmed by a secret family compact with Spain, by which, in default of heirs-male of his own body, Ferdinand bequeathed to that crown the kingdom of Bohemia, without first consulting the wishes of that nation, and without regard to its right of free election. The many enemies, too, which by his reforms in Styria that prince had provoked among the Protestants, were very prejudicial to his interests in Bohemia; and some Styrian emigrants, who had taken refuge there, bringing with them into their adopted country hearts overflowing with a desire of revenge, were particularly active in exciting the flame of revolt. Thus ill-affected did Ferdinand find the Bohemians, when he succeeded Matthias.

So bad an understanding between the nation and the candidate for the throne, would have raised a storm even in the most peaceable succession; how much more so at the present moment, before the ardour of insurrection had cooled; when the nation had just recovered its dignity, and reasserted its rights; when they still held arms in their hands, and the consciousness of unity had awakened an enthusiastic reliance on their own strength; when by past success, by the promises of foreign assistance, and by visionary expectations of the future, their courage had been raised to an undoubting confidence. Disregarding the rights already conferred on Ferdinand, the Estates declared the throne vacant, and their right of election entirely unfettered. All hopes of their peaceful submission were at an end, and if Ferdinand wished still to wear the crown of Bohemia, he must choose between purchasing it at the sacrifice of all that would make a crown desirable, or winning it sword in hand.

But with what means was it to be won? Turn his eyes where he would, the fire of revolt was burning. Silesia had already joined the insurgents in Bohemia; Moravia was on the point of following its example. In Upper and Lower Austria the spirit of liberty was awake, as it had been under Rodolph, and the Estates refused to do homage. Hungary was menaced with an inroad by Prince Bethlen Gabor, on the side of Transylvania; a secret arming among the Turks spread consternation among the provinces to the eastward; and, to complete his perplexities, the Protestants also, in his hereditary dominions, stimulated by the general example, were again raising their heads. In that quarter, their numbers were overwhelming; in most places they had possession of the revenues which Ferdinand would need for the maintenance of the war. The neutral began to waver, the faithful to be discouraged, the turbulent alone to be animated and confident. One half of Germany encouraged the rebels, the other inactively awaited the issue; Spanish assistance was still very remote. The moment which had brought him every thing, threatened also to deprive him of all.

And when he now, yielding to the stern law of necessity, made overtures to the Bohemian rebels, all his proposals for peace were insolently rejected. Count Thurn, at the head of an army, entered Moravia to bring this province, which alone continued to waver, to a decision. The appearance of their friends is the signal of revolt for the Moravian Protestants. Bruenn is taken, the remainder of the country yields with free will, throughout the province government and religion are changed. Swelling as it flows, the torrent of rebellion pours down upon Austria, where a party, holding similar sentiments, receives it with a joyful concurrence. Henceforth, there should be no more distinctions of religion; equality of rights should be guaranteed to all Christian churches. They hear that a foreign force has been invited into the country to oppress the Bohemians. Let them be sought out, and the enemies of liberty pursued to the ends of the earth. Not an arm is raised in defence of the Archduke, and the rebels, at length, encamp before Vienna to besiege their sovereign.

Ferdinand had sent his children from Gratz, where they were no longer safe, to the Tyrol; he himself awaited the insurgents in his capital. A handful of soldiers was all he could oppose to the enraged multitude; these few were without pay or provisions, and therefore little to be depended on. Vienna was unprepared for a long siege. The party of the Protestants, ready at any moment to join the Bohemians, had the preponderance in the city; those in the country had already begun to levy troops against him. Already, in imagination, the Protestant populace saw the Emperor shut up in a monastery, his territories divided, and his children educated as Protestants. Confiding in secret, and surrounded by public enemies, he saw the chasm every moment widening to engulf his hopes and even himself. The Bohemian bullets were already falling upon the imperial palace, when sixteen Austrian barons forcibly entered his chamber, and inveighing against him with loud and bitter reproaches, endeavoured to force him into a confederation with the Bohemians. One of them, seizing him by the button of his doublet, demanded, in a tone of menace, "Ferdinand, wilt thou sign it?"

Who would not be pardoned had he wavered in this frightful situation? Yet Ferdinand still remembered the dignity of a Roman emperor. No alternative seemed left to him but an immediate flight or submission; laymen urged him to the one, priests to the other. If he abandoned the city, it would fall into the enemy's hands; with Vienna, Austria was lost; with Austria, the imperial throne. Ferdinand abandoned not his capital, and as little would he hear of conditions.

The Archduke is still engaged in altercation with the deputed barons, when all at once a sound of trumpets is heard in the palace square. Terror and astonishment take possession of all present; a fearful report pervades the palace; one deputy after another disappears. Many of the nobility and the citizens hastily take refuge in the camp of Thurn. This sudden change is effected by a regiment of Dampierre's cuirassiers, who at that moment marched into the city to defend the Archduke. A body of infantry soon followed; reassured by their appearance, several of the Roman Catholic citizens, and even the students themselves, take up arms. A report which arrived just at the same time from Bohemia made his deliverance complete. The Flemish general, Bucquoi, had totally defeated Count Mansfeld at Budweiss, and was marching upon Prague. The Bohemians hastily broke up their camp before Vienna to protect their own capital.

And now also the passes were free which the enemy had taken possession of, in order to obstruct Ferdinand's progress to his coronation at Frankfort. If the accession to the imperial throne was important for the plans of the King of Hungary, it was of still greater consequence at the present moment, when his nomination as Emperor would afford the most unsuspicious and decisive proof of the dignity of his person, and of the justice of his cause, while, at the same time, it would give him a hope of support from the Empire. But the same cabal which opposed him in his hereditary dominions, laboured also to counteract him in his canvass for the imperial dignity. No Austrian prince, they maintained, ought to ascend the throne; least of all Ferdinand, the bigoted persecutor of their religion, the slave of Spain and of the Jesuits. To prevent this, the crown had been offered, even during the lifetime of Matthias, to the Duke of Bavaria, and on his refusal, to the Duke of Savoy. As some difficulty was experienced in settling with the latter the conditions of acceptance, it was sought, at all events, to delay the election till some decisive blow in Austria or Bohemia should annihilate all the hopes of Ferdinand, and incapacitate him from any competition for this dignity. The members of the Union left no stone unturned to gain over from Ferdinand the Electorate of Saxony, which was bound to Austrian interests; they represented to this court the dangers with which the Protestant religion, and even the constitution of the empire, were threatened by the principles of this prince and his Spanish alliance. By the elevation of Ferdinand to the imperial throne, Germany, they further asserted, would be involved in the private quarrels of this prince, and bring upon itself the arms of Bohemia. But in spite of all opposing influences, the day of election was fixed, Ferdinand summoned to it as lawful king of Bohemia, and his electoral vote, after a fruitless resistance on the part of the Bohemian Estates, acknowledged to be good. The votes of the three ecclesiastical electorates were for him, Saxony was favourable to him, Brandenburg made no opposition, and a decided majority declared him Emperor in 1619. Thus he saw the most doubtful of his crowns placed first of all on his head; but a few days after he lost that which he had reckoned among the most certain of his possessions. While he was thus elected Emperor in Frankfort, he was in Prague deprived of the Bohemian throne.

Almost all of his German hereditary dominions had in the meantime entered into a formidable league with the Bohemians, whose insolence now exceeded all bounds. In a general Diet, the latter, on the 17th of August, 1619, proclaimed the Emperor an enemy to the Bohemian religion and liberties, who by his pernicious counsels had alienated from them the affections of the late Emperor, had furnished troops to oppress them, had given their country as a prey to foreigners, and finally, in contravention of the national rights, had bequeathed the crown, by a secret compact, to Spain: they therefore declared that he had forfeited whatever title he might otherwise have had to the crown, and immediately proceeded to a new election. As this sentence was pronounced by Protestants, their choice could not well fall upon a Roman Catholic prince, though, to save appearances, some voices were raised for Bavaria and Savoy. But the violent religious animosities which divided the evangelical and the reformed parties among the Protestants, impeded for some time the election even of a Protestant king; till at last the address and activity of the Calvinists carried the day from the numerical superiority of the Lutherans.

Among all the princes who were competitors for this dignity, the Elector Palatine Frederick V. had the best grounded claims on the confidence and gratitude of the Bohemians; and among them all, there was no one in whose case the private interests of particular Estates, and the attachment of the people, seemed to be justified by so many considerations of state. Frederick V. was of a free and lively spirit, of great goodness of heart, and regal liberality. He was the head of the Calvinistic party in Germany, the leader of the Union, whose resources were at his disposal, a near relation of the Duke of Bavaria, and a son-in-law of the King of Great Britain, who might lend him his powerful support. All these considerations were prominently and successfully brought forward by the Calvinists, and Frederick V. was chosen king by the Assembly at Prague, amidst prayers and tears of joy.

The whole proceedings of the Diet at Prague had been premeditated, and Frederick himself had taken too active a share in the matter to feel at all surprised at the offer made to him by the Bohemians. But now the immediate glitter of this throne dazzled him, and the magnitude both of his elevation and his delinquency made his weak mind to tremble. After the usual manner of pusillanimous spirits, he sought to confirm himself in his purpose by the opinions of others; but these opinions had no weight with him when they ran counter to his own cherished wishes. Saxony and Bavaria, of whom he sought advice, all his brother electors, all who compared the magnitude of the design with his capacities and resources, warned him of the danger into which he was about to rush. Even King James of England preferred to see his son-in-law deprived of this crown, than that the sacred majesty of kings should be outraged by so dangerous a precedent. But of what avail was the voice of prudence against the seductive glitter of a crown? In the moment of boldest determination, when they are indignantly rejecting the consecrated branch of a race which had governed them for two centuries, a free people throws itself into his arms. Confiding in his courage, they choose him as their leader in the dangerous career of glory and liberty. To him, as to its born champion, an oppressed religion looks for shelter and support against its persecutors. Could he have the weakness to listen to his fears, and to betray the cause of religion and liberty? This religion proclaims to him its own preponderance, and the weakness of its rival,—two-thirds of the power of Austria are now in arms against Austria itself, while a formidable confederacy, already formed in Transylvania, would, by a hostile attack, further distract even the weak remnant of its power. Could inducements such as these fail to awaken his ambition, or such hopes to animate and inflame his resolution?

A few moments of calm consideration would have sufficed to show the danger of the undertaking, and the comparative worthlessness of the prize. But the temptation spoke to his feelings; the warning only to his reason. It was his misfortune that his nearest and most influential counsellors espoused the side of his passions. The aggrandizement of their master's power opened to the ambition and avarice of his Palatine servants an unlimited field for their gratification; this anticipated triumph of their church kindled the ardour of the Calvinistic fanatic. Could a mind so weak as that of Ferdinand resist the delusions of his counsellors, who exaggerated his resources and his strength, as much as they underrated those of his enemies; or the exhortations of his preachers, who announced the effusions of their fanatical zeal as the immediate inspiration of heaven? The dreams of astrology filled his mind with visionary hopes; even love conspired, with its irresistible fascination, to complete the seduction. "Had you," demanded the Electress, "confidence enough in yourself to accept the hand of a king's daughter, and have you misgivings about taking a crown which is voluntarily offered you? I would rather eat bread at thy kingly table, than feast at thy electoral board."

Frederick accepted the Bohemian crown. The coronation was celebrated with unexampled pomp at Prague, for the nation displayed all its riches in honour of its own work. Silesia and Moravia, the adjoining provinces to Bohemia, followed their example, and did homage to Frederick. The reformed faith was enthroned in all the churches of the kingdom; the rejoicings were unbounded, their attachment to their new king bordered on adoration. Denmark and Sweden, Holland and Venice, and several of the Dutch states, acknowledged him as lawful sovereign, and Frederick now prepared to maintain his new acquisition.

His principal hopes rested on Prince Bethlen Gabor of Transylvania. This formidable enemy of Austria, and of the Roman Catholic church, not content with the principality which, with the assistance of the Turks, he had wrested from his legitimate prince, Gabriel Bathori, gladly seized this opportunity of aggrandizing himself at the expense of Austria, which had hesitated to acknowledge him as sovereign of Transylvania. An attack upon Hungary and Austria was concerted with the Bohemian rebels, and both armies were to unite before the capital. Meantime, Bethlen Gabor, under the mask of friendship, disguised the true object of his warlike preparations, artfully promising the Emperor to lure the Bohemians into the toils, by a pretended offer of assistance, and to deliver up to him alive the leaders of the insurrection. All at once, however, he appeared in a hostile attitude in Upper Hungary. Before him went terror, and devastation behind; all opposition yielded, and at Presburg he received the Hungarian crown. The Emperor's brother, who governed in Vienna, trembled for the capital. He hastily summoned General Bucquoi to his assistance, and the retreat of the Imperialists drew the Bohemians, a second time, before the walls of Vienna. Reinforced by twelve thousand Transylvanians, and soon after joined by the victorious army of Bethlen Gabor, they again menaced the capital with assault; all the country round Vienna was laid waste, the navigation of the Danube closed, all supplies cut off, and the horrors of famine were threatened. Ferdinand, hastily recalled to his capital by this urgent danger, saw himself a second time on the brink of ruin. But want of provisions, and the inclement weather, finally compelled the Bohemians to go into quarters, a defeat in Hungary recalled Bethlen Gabor, and thus once more had fortune rescued the Emperor.

In a few weeks the scene was changed, and by his prudence and activity Ferdinand improved his position as rapidly as Frederick, by indolence and impolicy, ruined his. The Estates of Lower Austria were regained to their allegiance by a confirmation of their privileges; and the few who still held out were declared guilty of `lese-majeste' and high treason. During the election of Frankfort, he had contrived, by personal representations, to win over to his cause the ecclesiastical electors, and also Maximilian, Duke of Bavaria, at Munich. The whole issue of the war, the fate of Frederick and the Emperor, were now dependent on the part which the Union and the League should take in the troubles of Bohemia. It was evidently of importance to all the Protestants of Germany that the King of Bohemia should be supported, while it was equally the interest of the Roman Catholics to prevent the ruin of the Emperor. If the Protestants succeeded in Bohemia, all the Roman Catholic princes in Germany might tremble for their possessions; if they failed, the Emperor would give laws to Protestant Germany. Thus Ferdinand put the League, Frederick the Union, in motion. The ties of relationship and a personal attachment to the Emperor, his brother-in-law, with whom he had been educated at Ingolstadt, zeal for the Roman Catholic religion, which seemed to be in the most imminent peril, and the suggestions of the Jesuits, combined with the suspicious movements of the Union, moved the Duke of Bavaria, and all the princes of the League, to make the cause of Ferdinand their own.

According to the terms of a treaty with the Emperor, which assured to the Duke of Bavaria compensation for all the expenses of the war, or the losses he might sustain, Maximilian took, with full powers, the command of the troops of the League, which were ordered to march to the assistance of the Emperor against the Bohemian rebels. The leaders of the Union, instead of delaying by every means this dangerous coalition of the League with the Emperor, did every thing in their power to accelerate it. Could they, they thought, but once drive the Roman Catholic League to take an open part in the Bohemian war, they might reckon on similar measures from all the members and allies of the Union. Without some open step taken by the Roman Catholics against the Union, no effectual confederacy of the Protestant powers was to be looked for. They seized, therefore, the present emergency of the troubles in Bohemia to demand from the Roman Catholics the abolition of their past grievances, and full security for the future exercise of their religion. They addressed this demand, which was moreover couched in threatening language, to the Duke of Bavaria, as the head of the Roman Catholics, and they insisted on an immediate and categorical answer. Maximilian might decide for or against them, still their point was gained; his concession, if he yielded, would deprive the Roman Catholic party of its most powerful protector; his refusal would arm the whole Protestant party, and render inevitable a war in which they hoped to be the conquerors. Maximilian, firmly attached to the opposite party from so many other considerations, took the demands of the Union as a formal declaration of hostilities, and quickened his preparations. While Bavaria and the League were thus arming in the Emperor's cause, negotiations for a subsidy were opened with the Spanish court. All the difficulties with which the indolent policy of that ministry met this demand were happily surmounted by the imperial ambassador at Madrid, Count Khevenhuller. In addition to a subsidy of a million of florins, which from time to time were doled out by this court, an attack upon the Lower Palatinate, from the side of the Spanish Netherlands, was at the same time agreed upon.

During these attempts to draw all the Roman Catholic powers into the League, every exertion was made against the counter-league of the Protestants. To this end, it was important to alarm the Elector of Saxony and the other Evangelical powers, and accordingly the Union were diligent in propagating a rumour that the preparations of the League had for their object to deprive them of the ecclesiastical foundations they had secularized. A written assurance to the contrary calmed the fears of the Duke of Saxony, whom moreover private jealousy of the Palatine, and the insinuations of his chaplain, who was in the pay of Austria, and mortification at having been passed over by the Bohemians in the election to the throne, strongly inclined to the side of Austria. The fanaticism of the Lutherans could never forgive the reformed party for having drawn, as they expressed it, so many fair provinces into the gulf of Calvinism, and rejecting the Roman Antichrist only to make way for an Helvetian one.

While Ferdinand used every effort to improve the unfavourable situation of his affairs, Frederick was daily injuring his good cause. By his close and questionable connexion with the Prince of Transylvania, the open ally of the Porte, he gave offence to weak minds; and a general rumour accused him of furthering his own ambition at the expense of Christendom, and arming the Turks against Germany. His inconsiderate zeal for the Calvinistic scheme irritated the Lutherans of Bohemia, his attacks on image-worship incensed the Papists of this kingdom against him. New and oppressive imposts alienated the affections of all his subjects. The disappointed hopes of the Bohemian nobles cooled their zeal; the absence of foreign succours abated their confidence. Instead of devoting himself with untiring energies to the affairs of his kingdom, Frederick wasted his time in amusements; instead of filling his treasury by a wise economy, he squandered his revenues by a needless theatrical pomp, and a misplaced munificence. With a light-minded carelessness, he did but gaze at himself in his new dignity, and in the ill-timed desire to enjoy his crown, he forgot the more pressing duty of securing it on his head.

But greatly as men had erred in their opinion of him, Frederick himself had not less miscalculated his foreign resources. Most of the members of the Union considered the affairs of Bohemia as foreign to the real object of their confederacy; others, who were devoted to him, were overawed by fear of the Emperor. Saxony and Hesse Darmstadt had already been gained over by Ferdinand; Lower Austria, on which side a powerful diversion had been looked for, had made its submission to the Emperor; and Bethlen Gabor had concluded a truce with him. By its embassies, the court of Vienna had induced Denmark to remain inactive, and to occupy Sweden in a war with the Poles. The republic of Holland had enough to do to defend itself against the arms of the Spaniards; Venice and Saxony remained inactive; King James of England was overreached by the artifice of Spain. One friend after another withdrew; one hope vanished after another—so rapidly in a few months was every thing changed.

In the mean time, the leaders of the Union assembled an army;—the Emperor and the League did the same. The troops of the latter were assembled under the banners of Maximilian at Donauwerth, those of the Union at Ulm, under the Margrave of Anspach. The decisive moment seemed at length to have arrived which was to end these long dissensions by a vigorous blow, and irrevocably to settle the relation of the two churches in Germany. Anxiously on the stretch was the expectation of both parties. How great then was their astonishment when suddenly the intelligence of peace arrived, and both armies separated without striking a blow!

The intervention of France effected this peace, which was equally acceptable to both parties. The French cabinet, no longer swayed by the counsels of Henry the Great, and whose maxims of state were perhaps not applicable to the present condition of that kingdom, was now far less alarmed at the preponderance of Austria, than of the increase which would accrue to the strength of the Calvinists, if the Palatine house should be able to retain the throne of Bohemia. Involved at the time in a dangerous conflict with its own Calvinistic subjects, it was of the utmost importance to France that the Protestant faction in Bohemia should be suppressed before the Huguenots could copy their dangerous example. In order therefore to facilitate the Emperor's operations against the Bohemians, she offered her mediation to the Union and the League, and effected this unexpected treaty, of which the main article was, "That the Union should abandon all interference in the affairs of Bohemia, and confine the aid which they might afford to Frederick the Fifth, to his Palatine territories." To this disgraceful treaty, the Union were moved by the firmness of Maximilian, and the fear of being pressed at once by the troops of the League, and a new Imperial army which was on its march from the Netherlands.

The whole force of Bavaria and the League was now at the disposal of the Emperor to be employed against the Bohemians, who by the pacification of Ulm were abandoned to their fate. With a rapid movement, and before a rumour of the proceedings at Ulm could reach there, Maximilian appeared in Upper Austria, when the Estates, surprised and unprepared for an enemy, purchased the Emperor's pardon by an immediate and unconditional submission. In Lower Austria, the duke formed a junction with the troops from the Low Countries under Bucquoi, and without loss of time the united Imperial and Bavarian forces, amounting to 50,000 men, entered Bohemia. All the Bohemian troops, which were dispersed over Lower Austria and Moravia, were driven before them; every town which attempted resistance was quickly taken by storm; others, terrified by the report of the punishment inflicted on these, voluntarily opened their gates; nothing in short interrupted the impetuous career of Maximilian. The Bohemian army, commanded by the brave Prince Christian of Anhalt, retreated to the neighbourhood of Prague; where, under the walls of the city, Maximilian offered him battle.

The wretched condition in which he hoped to surprise the insurgents, justified the rapidity of the duke's movements, and secured him the victory. Frederick's army did not amount to 30,000 men. Eight thousand of these were furnished by the Prince of Anhalt; 10,000 were Hungarians, whom Bethlen Gabor had despatched to his assistance. An inroad of the Elector of Saxony upon Lusatia, had cut off all succours from that country, and from Silesia; the pacification of Austria put an end to all his expectations from that quarter; Bethlen Gabor, his most powerful ally, remained inactive in Transylvania; the Union had betrayed his cause to the Emperor. Nothing remained to him but his Bohemians; and they were without goodwill to his cause, and without unity and courage. The Bohemian magnates were indignant that German generals should be put over their heads; Count Mansfeld remained in Pilsen, at a distance from the camp, to avoid the mortification of serving under Anhalt and Hohenlohe. The soldiers, in want of necessaries, became dispirited; and the little discipline that was observed, gave occasion to bitter complaints from the peasantry. It was in vain that Frederick made his appearance in the camp, in the hope of reviving the courage of the soldiers by his presence, and of kindling the emulation of the nobles by his example.

The Bohemians had begun to entrench themselves on the White Mountain near Prague, when they were attacked by the Imperial and Bavarian armies, on the 8th November, 1620. In the beginning of the action, some advantages were gained by the cavalry of the Prince of Anhalt; but the superior numbers of the enemy soon neutralized them. The charge of the Bavarians and Walloons was irresistible. The Hungarian cavalry was the first to retreat. The Bohemian infantry soon followed their example; and the Germans were at last carried along with them in the general flight. Ten cannons, composing the whole of Frederick's artillery, were taken by the enemy; four thousand Bohemians fell in the flight and on the field; while of the Imperialists and soldiers of the League only a few hundred were killed. In less than an hour this decisive action was over.

Frederick was seated at table in Prague, while his army was thus cut to pieces. It is probable that he had not expected the attack on this day, since he had ordered an entertainment for it. A messenger summoned him from table, to show him from the walls the whole frightful scene. He requested a cessation of hostilities for twenty-four hours for deliberation; but eight was all the Duke of Bavaria would allow him. Frederick availed himself of these to fly by night from the capital, with his wife, and the chief officers of his army.

This flight was so hurried, that the Prince of Anhalt left behind him his most private papers, and Frederick his crown. "I know now what I am," said this unfortunate prince to those who endeavoured to comfort him; "there are virtues which misfortune only can teach us, and it is in adversity alone that princes learn to know themselves."

Prague was not irretrievably lost when Frederick's pusillanimity abandoned it. The light troops of Mansfeld were still in Pilsen, and were not engaged in the action. Bethlen Gabor might at any moment have assumed an offensive attitude, and drawn off the Emperor's army to the Hungarian frontier. The defeated Bohemians might rally. Sickness, famine, and the inclement weather, might wear out the enemy; but all these hopes disappeared before the immediate alarm. Frederick dreaded the fickleness of the Bohemians, who might probably yield to the temptation to purchase, by the surrender of his person, the pardon of the Emperor.

Thurn, and those of this party who were in the same condemnation with him, found it equally inexpedient to await their destiny within the walls of Prague. They retired towards Moravia, with a view of seeking refuge in Transylvania. Frederick fled to Breslau, where, however, he only remained a short time. He removed from thence to the court of the Elector of Brandenburg, and finally took shelter in Holland.

The battle of Prague had decided the fate of Bohemia. Prague surrendered the next day to the victors; the other towns followed the example of the capital. The Estates did homage without conditions, and the same was done by those of Silesia and Moravia. The Emperor allowed three months to elapse, before instituting any inquiry into the past. Reassured by this apparent clemency, many who, at first, had fled in terror appeared again in the capital. All at once, however, the storm burst forth; forty-eight of the most active among the insurgents were arrested on the same day and hour, and tried by an extraordinary commission, composed of native Bohemians and Austrians. Of these, twenty-seven, and of the common people an immense number, expired on the scaffold. The absenting offenders were summoned to appear to their trial, and failing to do so, condemned to death, as traitors and offenders against his Catholic Majesty, their estates confiscated, and their names affixed to the gallows. The property also of the rebels who had fallen in the field was seized. This tyranny might have been borne, as it affected individuals only, and while the ruin of one enriched another; but more intolerable was the oppression which extended to the whole kingdom, without exception. All the Protestant preachers were banished from the country; the Bohemians first, and afterwards those of Germany. The `Letter of Majesty', Ferdinand tore with his own hand, and burnt the seal. Seven years after the battle of Prague, the toleration of the Protestant religion within the kingdom was entirely revoked. But whatever violence the Emperor allowed himself against the religious privileges of his subjects, he carefully abstained from interfering with their political constitution; and while he deprived them of the liberty of thought, he magnanimously left them the prerogative of taxing themselves.

The victory of the White Mountain put Ferdinand in possession of all his dominions. It even invested him with greater authority over them than his predecessors enjoyed, since their allegiance had been unconditionally pledged to him, and no Letter of Majesty now existed to limit his sovereignty. All his wishes were now gratified, to a degree surpassing his most sanguine expectations.

It was now in his power to dismiss his allies, and disband his army. If he was just, there was an end of the war—if he was both magnanimous and just, punishment was also at an end. The fate of Germany was in his hands; the happiness and misery of millions depended on the resolution he should take. Never was so great a decision resting on a single mind; never did the blindness of one man produce so much ruin.

Milton Keynes UK
Ingram Content Group UK Ltd.
UKHW031049120324
439302UK00006B/450